Communication & Beyond

Central Technical College, Brisbane.

Communication & Beyond

Rodney G. Miller

Parula Press

Communication & Beyond

Copyright © Rodney G Miller 2022

All rights reserved. No portion of this book may be reproduced, distributed, or transmitted in any form by any means without the prior written permission of the publisher, except brief quotations within reviews and specified noncommercial uses permitted by copyright law. For permission requests, write to "Attention: Permissions" at: Parula Press, 1971 Western Avenue #147, Albany, NY 12203, United States of America

Notice: Every effort was made to trace the holders of copyright material. If you have any information concerning copyright material in this book, please contact the publishers at the address above.

Cover Image: Brisbane Central Technical College (former) (2008)
now QUT Gardens Point Administration
Credit: Heritage branch staff, Wikimedia Commons CCA 3.0 Unported

Frontispiece Image: Central Technical College in Brisbane (former B Block), ca. 1931
Credit: Unknown, https://commons.wikimedia.org/wiki/Template:PD-1996 and
https://commons.wikimedia.org/wiki/Template:PD-AustraliaGov

Cataloging-in-Publication Data
Name: Miller, Rodney G., author
Title: *Communication & Beyond*
Description: Albany, NY: Parula Press, [2022]
Rodney G. Miller; source notes, bibliography
Subjects: LCSH: 1. Communication – Study Teaching – Australia
2. Education, Higher – Australia – History
3. Teachers – Biography

ISBN: 978-1-7374895-2-8 (hardback)

Library of Congress Control Number: 2022904511

For Thomas C. Dixon AM, Professor Emeritus, QUT,

who provided many opportunities for this "bloke studying rhetoric,"

and for generous colleagues and friends, who taught me so much

Table of Contents

Preface...ix
1: Everything Felt New..1
2. Into the Academy at QIT...12
3. National Professional Developments..............................25
4: Communication Meaning..36
5. Doing It..48
Source Notes..59
Bibliography...65
Acknowledgments...70
About the Author...71

Preface

From the 1970s onwards, Australia experienced remarkable changes in the commercial, government, and nonprofit sectors. How organizations related to both the community and their employees changed progressively, requiring more frequent and more personal interaction. Together with growth in the arts, mass media, telecommunications, and other areas, these changes and more put a spotlight on communication.

To help address new and enduring communication challenges throughout the nation, academics in Australian higher education designed and taught a variety of degree-level courses directed to enhance the understanding and practice of communication. These efforts ushered in a new dawn of communication education. Among the new courses for study was a premier degree in communication established at Queensland University of Technology (QUT), in Brisbane, Australia.

For more than two decades as an academic and then as an administrator, QUT provided tremendous opportunities to help bridge communication study, teaching, and practice. Touching on social currents from the mid-1970s to the early 21st century, **Communication & Beyond** chronicles my reflections on some people, principles, and practices responsible for advancing communication education and external relations initiatives at QUT and beyond. I've since drawn on the QUT experience to lead the advancement of the innovative education in universities within the United States and internationally.

This booklet records reflections on one stage in the evolution of communication study and teaching in Australia. Mostly described is what I've directly encountered, rather than the many developments in the study and teaching of communication during subsequent years. While occupied leading initiatives to increase resources for the academy, very apparent though is a continuously expanding and exciting future that's possible for anyone equipped to put communication understandings into practice.

Rodney G. Miller

1: Everything Felt New

During the early 1970s, Australia saw a strong expansion of higher education[1] at a time of tremendous change in the national economy, politics, and daily life. The nation experienced a burgeoning of professional education programs. Change and growth in communication education mirrored the rapidly expanding higher education sector. These years saw spectacular growth in higher education communication departments, similar in some ways to what had occurred previously in North America.

Amid economic changes after World War II, the expectations and priorities of both older and newer generations of Australians were in flux. Worldwide, adjustments in lifestyles, social norms, and culture were quickly disseminated into households through an expanding range and reach of mass media. In families and in the workplace, changes in interpersonal communication were disruptive of some social norms.

This was a time when middle-aged and older Australians, who had experienced economic depression and world wars, seemed to look for stability and security. In contrast, their children and grandchildren, who were to enroll in the newly developing communication courses, were keen to explore new approaches to personal life and to take on new professional roles. Concurrently, population growth and expansions in manufacturing, mining, construction, technology, and other areas were occurring, contributing to a demand for entrepreneurial and community service initiatives that increased the range of employment opportunities in the private and public sectors.

Enhanced Communication

For many of these roles, Australia needed people with enhanced communication ability to advance the initiatives. People skilled in communication were in demand for work in advertising, broadcasting, business, film, government, journalism, nonprofits, public relations, teaching, and emerging technologies, along with many other areas. Graduates of communication degree courses were soon to advance into responsible roles, initially as "communication doers," then as strategists and advisers to leaders, and progressively as leaders of companies, government, and nonprofits.

Communication teachers and researchers certainly viewed communication as consequential to these roles and more broadly to human affairs.

A widely shared belief inside and outside the academy was that efforts in communication study and teaching might help develop "better communication." Various leaders in business, government, and the professions, including the news media, were seeking out communication academics for comment and insight on ways to enhance communication, to develop better relationships in many spheres of life. This suggested that some improvements to mutual understandings among people were possible.

The emergence of new communication technologies and workplace practices, along with a curiosity about changes in the social framework, institutions, workplace interactions, and communication processes stimulated many studies of interpersonal and mass communication, as well as mass media institutions. It was a vibrant time to be teaching and researching communication.

Political Change

In the early 1970s, Australians were working through the experience of a reformist Labor Government led by Gough Whitlam, which was vigorously legislating in a wide range of areas, stimulating rapid social change. At the end of 1975, a constitutional crisis suddenly put the brakes on the federal government's reform agenda. When Gough Whitlam was sacked by the Queen's representative, using a reserve power put in place in Queen Victoria's time, social disagreements took center stage. This caused the public relations lecturer at QIT to write:

> Australia today is a badly shaken society; there are few indications of a return to stability. Tremors that now unsettle the political structure will eventually undermine the foundations of all institutions. These shock waves, already being felt in business and education, originate in the ideas, beliefs, enthusiasms and biases of people and can be countered only by re-establishing in the public mind the worth of each institution. And this counteractivity evokes public relations, which must do its work in an ambience of mounting scepticism of all information, whatever the source.[2]

Inarguably, these were uncertain times, although the suggestion of an anticipated demise of Australian institutions was likely accentuated by sensitivities that derived from the writer's United States origin.

Many academics in Australia were deeply disappointed by the turn in political events. But companies and government were increasingly attentive to the role that communication might serve to meet an increasing expectation that organizations communicate better, especially through their formative customer relations and social responsibility efforts.

Communication was often touted as the solution to many challenges. It was inherent in most activities and seemed everywhere to be a concern. Yet little clarity pertained on the many different meanings with which the word was used in the different provinces of the academy, news media, and interpersonally. Partly for this reason, it was as clear to Australian educators as to their counterparts elsewhere in the world, that communication study was "wildly heterogeneous."[3] From established disciplines, academics could reach into this "new" area of study and application "to ask new questions" and "break out of approaches that [were] standard" in established disciplines.[4]

Communication Education

At first, the higher education offerings of any scale under the banner of communication were pre-degree courses in oral and written communication skills. When charged to tackle the need to dramatically increase the level, range, and scale of communication teaching and research, Australian academics saw this as an opportunity. Faced with a need to grow communication programs throughout the country, a problem-solving approach used was to review what communication-related occupations were likely to be needed then and in the future in the community.

Shaping new offerings from what was virtually a "blank page" might include exploration of the courses established elsewhere, particularly in North America, and then drafting approaches and directions to meet local or regional needs. These efforts tended to incorporate or create whatever might need to be done differently, to be most appropriate to the Australian context.

Also partly driving the educational developments were worldwide trends in the 1960s and later decades to reassess norms previously taken for granted, along with an Australian inclination to question accepted traditions. At times, Australians will express a contrariness in a variety of ways to challenge established overseas approaches. Later, during the delivery and refinement of the educational offerings, within the mix also was empathy with some of the early communication students, who voiced their wish for Australian teaching materials that could deal with Australian differences and sensitivities, especially through Australian case studies.

Concerns and Growth

Arguably, communication teaching did not develop only as some type of amalgamation of the efforts of the British and American academies. Although Australian communication teachers and researchers were generally familiar with overseas education programs and publications, there were many impulses to do things differently, and hopefully better. Incorporating whatever local difference might require was not new to Australia. This was consistent with sentiments of the early Australian writers and artists in the nation's modern history, who developed new voices in a colonial and post-colonial country. Though conscious of the nature of their largely British and European origins, these writers and artists created works incorporating the differences of the Australian landscape, lifestyle, and ways of thinking—even though British reviewers long persisted in comparing Australian creative outputs with the norms of British or European icons and culture.

Teachers and researchers certainly sought to incorporate in their programs what was perceived as well-grounded from the contemporary efforts overseas, but there were inherent limits on this. While teaching oral communication, it was obvious, for example, how applicable or not were the techniques of famous British and North American public speakers, to illustrate what was appropriate for Australian public address.

Differences to be considered for the Australian context were just as obvious when teaching advertising, public relations, journalism, broadcasting, or other aspects of communication—likewise, the nature of communication networks or audiences, and the operating structures and principles of mass media institutions, or politics, or business practices. Virtually all areas of communication require understandings and an embrace of sometimes very large differences from what pertains overseas.

Of some influence also was a growing sense of nationalism and republicanism that was bubbling in the country. The Australian film director Bruce Beresford had enjoyed initial box-office success with *The Adventures of Barry McKenzie* (1972) and *Barry McKenzie Holds His Own* (1974). Both films were so badly received critically that Beresford later said they were detrimental to his career. But this was a time when, along with other creative Australians, Beresford was shaping ideas for productions that were to become part of a new wave of the Australian film industry. It was in 1976, at the invitation of QIT colleague Bruce Molloy, that Beresford visited the campus and gave a talk that helped to consolidate feelings that something interestingly different was happening in a second act of Australian filmmaking.[5]

Interpersonal Difference

Within daily interpersonal communication, the different character and varieties of Australians' conversational language were unlikely to be lost on anyone—to be able to communicate! Memorably, a visiting British linguistics academic during his conference presentation in 1980 made this clear. Driving cross-country to the conference from the east coast to Adelaide, he had stopped at a petrol station somewhere in western New South Wales far from anywhere, which could be a lot of places. He noticed that the petrol station cashier had a sign on the wall behind him. At the top of the sign in large letters was the bold offer "We cash cheques," and at the base of the sign, in equally large letters, was the comforting statement, "We do." But in between these two lines of words was a cartoon-like, large drawing of a pig's pink rear-end.

Very likely, every Australian who came into the cashier read the sign's message as, "We cash cheques / [pig's ar*e]/ we do"–which meant "No cheques cashed." The British academic clearly got the meaning. He excitedly shared the photo he'd taken of the sign to make his point about Aussie communication, highlighting the use of slang, image, and words. He also recalled his cryptic conversation with the Aussie cashier. The cashier wondered what all the fuss was about, that this "Pommy" wanted to photograph his sign. The British visitor's impressive intercultural skill highlights some undercurrents in much Australian communication.

Australian Context

The context for communication teaching and research was inevitably influenced by Australians' characteristic use of words, images, vernacular, and cultural difference. During everyday Aussie talk, anyone with an interest in communication was well primed, for example, to be curious about exploring language, often encountering analogy, rhyming substitutions, abbreviation, imaginative omission, and lots of figurative language.

Not everywhere in the world will you hear the phrase "like a lizard drinking," with everyone around you understanding this translates to "busy"–because a lizard lies "flat out" busily drinking at the billabong... and it's commonly known that a billabong is a particular type of watering hole and not a surfing reference, despite the confusion created by this also becoming a popular brand-name for surfing gear and clothing.

Or how many people do non-Australians know who, out of the blue, refer to a best friend and/or spouse as "china plate," or just "china," or "plate"? Of course, Cockneys and Aussies know what this is because there is a rhyme with "mate," and everyone knows what that means, right!

These are some of what are better known among quite a large trove of Australian/Oz-talk–now, that's "clear as mud" someone from overseas might say, but will any non-Australian routinely put these and many more language adaptations and adoptions one after another continuously in every sentence spoken? No wonder that John O'Grady, writing under his pseudonym Nino Culotta, sold so many copies of *They're a Weird Mob*–a 1957 comic novel about an Italian immigrant to Australia trying to work all this out. And then there is Frank Hardy's irreverently humorous satire, *The Outcasts of Foolgarah*–which would require way too many more pages than the book itself to translate from Oz-talk, however imprecisely.

More broadly by analogy, and much less colloquially, Australian tone and substance were concerns for developing teaching and research efforts that would enable insights about communication. Of particular concern were any notable differences needed for communication practices, workplace experiences, or even observations about media ownership and industry structures in Australia that were different from what was observable overseas. Regardless of the light-hearted perspective or any casual quality in the vernacular of Australian communication, such as what the British linguist had observed or what other examples might suggest, the communication education efforts in the "polytechs" and colleges were serious business.

Professional Interests

Communication teachers and researchers sought to prepare new generations of students for their own life-long efforts in careers that would finish up helping to transform Australian society. The period from the early 1970s saw a new dawn of communication education.

Mostly, the academics who advanced these efforts were gregarious, interested in what another teacher, researcher, or practitioner might say about communication or think about one's own work. Academic gatherings and explorations of educational approaches occurred over many years, as outlined by Steven Maras and others.[6]

What stirred the professional interests of communication academics varied tremendously. For some, it was delight in the spoken word. Many had grown up valuing the power of the written word to move people. Nonverbal communication modes engaged others. Everyone was fascinated with a facet of communication, like bowerbirds devoted quite instinctively to making a particular bower better, with some collaborative research occurring in areas of mutual interest.

The individual interests of people who advanced the teaching and the research were inevitably influenced by the nation's legacy as former British colonies. In the decades following World War II, Australia was still defining itself as a more independent unified nation on the international stage.

One group of academics, within a subset of speech communication study and teaching, sought to expand the long history of generations of elocution teaching inherited mostly from Britain, with its system of education and performance. My mother, born early in the twentieth century, still fondly recalled in her 80s, the childhood experience with her younger sister of the Sunday afternoon concert of elocution recitations in the neighbor's larger drawing room or the local church hall.

By the 1970s, many of the educators still advancing this inheritance were well established, usually as teachers of speech and dramatic performance or teachers of trainee teachers. Some members of this cohort of communication academics in 1979-80 were to help found what was originally characterized as an association of tertiary communication academics—the *Australian Communication Association*, which later evolved into the *Australian and New Zealand Communication Association*.

Yet from the earliest stages of this new communication dawning and the foundation of this Association, the variety of interests of communication teachers and researchers was much wider and robust than just one or a few approaches.

Communication teachers and researchers were mainly employed in institutes of technology, or colleges of advanced education, or technical colleges throughout the nation, with relatively few in universities. Institutes of technology, much like the red-brick polytechnics in Britain, tended to be in the city center. Frequently, fifty percent or more of the students attending these inner-city institutes worked in the real world by day and attended classes part-time at night. Some students managed to work full-time while completing the annual requirement for the full-time course, for at least portions of their studies. They often brought to class real-world cases, questions, and challenge.

As the degree courses were developed, educators in these institutes and colleges of advanced education shrugged off occasionally encountered slights from some self-regarded guardians of knowledge in this era within the long-established "sandstone universities." Apparently, these folk sincerely believed that a so-called "second-tier" of tertiary education courses in the institutes and colleges was somehow less rigorous or valuable. Encountering such inferences just added to the determination of the academics in institutes and colleges to ensure programs were well-suited to what students and society seemed to want and need.

Degree-level Course

The first Australian degree-level course in Communication was established in 1974 at Queensland Institute of Technology (QIT), now Queensland University of Technology (QUT).[7] Tom Dixon and Bruce Molloy designed the course to award a Bachelor of Business (Communication), initially with professional strands in advertising and public relations.

Tom was appointed in 1967 by the head of the business school, Dr. Sidney S. Webb, whose PhD was from Ohio State. The school had two departments, Accountancy (headed by Merv Hoskins) and Management (headed by Dr. Jim Kable), with a section of General Studies (also named as "English and Social Science" by 1972)[8] reporting to Kable. Teachers from the General Studies Section serviced a number of Institute courses, with communication subjects focused mainly on writing and speaking in business or professional contexts. These subjects were variously named English, Business Communication,

Communication in Commerce, English Expression, Organisational Communication, Research and Communication, and Business English (which included "a discussion of the novel and drama as literary art forms").[9] In February 1975, the Communication Section was established within the Department of Management. QIT was led by Dr. Don Fraser (an engineer by profession) and the vision for the business school came from Webb, who within a few years was to die following a horse-riding accident on his farm.[10]

Tom's initial role was to teach oral and written communication to certificate through diploma students in business, engineering, built environment, and science, alongside John Knowles who had worked at QIT's predecessor institution, The Central Technical College. In 1968, Tom hired Bruce Molloy, with Keith Bain arriving soon after and Robert Kelly a year or so later.

Some early teachers of communication programs servicing professional disciplines of an institute of technology or a college of advanced education might have felt trapped within a service role.[11] At QIT initially, Tom and Bruce set about building coherent programs in communication in the developing service subjects for aspiring accountants, architects, engineers, scientists, town planners, or other professionals, to enhance oral and written communication understandings and abilities needed for practice.

An ebullient Australian patriot, Bruce had a wide range of interests focused on history, literature, and film. He later incorporated these interests within a subject he had developed on *Australian Studies* in the communication degree, where the lectures he invited me to provide included a set piece interpreting Australian art's representation of the Australian ethos. Bruce also developed a wide range of communication service subjects with the encouragement of the inaugural head of the Built Environment School, Eddie Codd, in all years and semesters of that School's vibrant programs–including within the creative courses in architecture, developed and led by Peter Cheney. These communication service subjects were so popular with students that many transferred to the B.Bus. (Communication) degree when it was established.[12]

In both this communication degree and throughout the communication service programs, Tom and Bruce were committed to the institution's mission to relate theory and practice. From the earliest at QIT and later at QUT, there were tussles to resolve appropriate emphases between pragmatic areas, such as organizational communication or professional strand subjects or even semantics/linguistics, and culture-based subjects, such as literature and the media. The tussles continuously influenced and often strengthened the design and teaching of subjects. This foreshadowed what would occur in universities over the following decades, in terms of ongoing debates and the emergence of cultural studies as a prominent paradigm.[13]

QIT Communication Course

Following Webb's death in the early 1970s, Tom and Bruce saw the prospects for English and Social Science as a service area as very limited within a business school now headed by a former head of accountancy, who evidenced a less strategic vision than Webb. As a former high school headmaster and mathematics teacher, Tom knew curriculum development and:

> ...he researched United States programs, coming up with a model initially based on the professional programs in PR and Advertising at Boston University...with advice on the structure from a visiting professor, Otto Lerbinger.[14]

Concurrently, Tom and Bruce advocated to the Institute's leaders for an upgrade to departmental status, through memberships of the QIT governing council and via a staff newsletter *Caduceus*, which Bruce had persuaded the Institute director to fund–and by lobbying media organizations and professional bodies of the advertising and public relations industries. The new QIT course was to be at degree level, and it was Robert Kelly who suggested the name "Communication" for the program, perhaps as early as 1969, saying it needed a name with some cachet.[15]

As Tom later told the story in his understated way, he said he went to the campus library and pulled off the library shelves the catalogs of communication degree programs in the United States, and progressively photocopied and adapted appropriate course descriptions. There were many more innovations made and complications overcome than his narrative implied, including multiple consultations within the academy and the professions, to develop a coherent program that secured accreditation approval. Tom and Bruce then recruited academic staff and students for the course.

Integrated Theory and Practice

From the outset, core studies of communication, sociology, and humanities were integrated in each semester of the communication degree. Theories of communication provided the foundation for teaching, integrated with principles from sociology and psychology, philosophy, and other areas. Sociology input was led by Phil Crowe, who also incorporated quantitative research methods within the communication study areas.

Complementary subjects in *Australian Studies* and *Business in Society* were based in history and philosophy, alongside the subjects for professional skills development in oral and written communication, public relations, and advertising. A priority in the integration of humanities and social science subjects was to:

> ...develop students' curiosity about their society and thereby build significant abilities in communication... Discussions... [were] critical/evaluative and stimulate[d] students to identify practical ways of getting others to think critically and constructively about the improvement of their society. Students soon recognize[d] that people communicating can assist one another to experience different values and value systems more fully.[16]

Each academic drew on individual disciplinary backgrounds in English, literature, linguistics, history, rhetoric, communication, sociology, psychology, or another area. Continuous liaison occurred with professional bodies to address practitioners' concerns, reservations, or criticism, and to incorporate pragmatic insights in the teaching program.

Early Expansion Nationally

In parallel, communication teaching programs were being developed elsewhere in Australia. A sense of these early times is captured in articles that outline the history of education in public relations[17] and journalism.[18] A course at Mitchell College of Advanced Education (now part of Charles Sturt University) in Bathurst, New South Wales was established in 1970 at the pre-degree level and was approved to award degrees in 1976.[19] This was a Bachelor of Arts (Communication), with professional strands in public relations and journalism:

> The year 1975 was important also for the establishment of concerted efforts in journalism education. At Mitchell College, Dave Potts spearheaded an effort for collaboration among colleagues interested in journalism, hosting 13 journalism educators to gather in December that year in Bathurst, to "make journalism education a respectable academic pursuit and an accepted part of the growth of professionalism in the Australian news industry."[20]

From early on within the QIT communication program, in addition to its strands in advertising and public relations, Tom Dixon had sought to incorporate journalism as a third professional strand. He had hired an experienced journalism educator, Ken Gompertz, who in 1975 at the Bathurst gathering became president of the newly created *Australian Association for Tertiary Education in Journalism* (AATEJ).[21] Among attendees at the gathering was John Henningham, who became Australia's first PhD in journalism and the nation's first professor of journalism, at The University of Queensland. He edited *Australian Journalism Review* for many years and subsequently developed *JSchool* as an independent journalism education institution.

Another important and different voice in journalism education around this time was Shelton Gunaratne, at Capricornia Institute of Advanced Education (now Central Queensland University) in Rockhampton, from 1976 to 1985. He offered fresh perspective on Asian media, highlighting the ethnocentric character of Australian journalism. His wide scholarship was further recognized in 2016 with The Asian Media Information and Communication Centre (AMIC) Asia Communication Award. This award acknowledged his "ground-breaking scholarship and intellectual contribution to Asian media and communication research."[22]

In both the QIT and Mitchell programs, a primary interest was to strengthen the systematic body of knowledge in the communication field. A shared aim was to improve both the intellectual rigor and professional skills of graduating students. Looking back at this time, Potts noted in 1977:

> NSW Institute of Technology had its first graduates of the Institute's degree program in communication at the end of last year. In Queensland, 13 students graduated from Queensland Institute of Technology's "Bachelor of Business" degree program in communication last year… In Western Australia, public relations is now being offered in a unit in the Western Australian Institute of Technology. The one-unit course is part of a Bachelor of Arts program and was launched last year with 14 students. In Victoria, a Certificate of Business Studies in public relations is being conducted by the Royal Melbourne Institute of Technology. The 21 students graduating at the end of last year will be the first to complete this three-year certificate course.[23]

Even as courses and resources for staffing expanded, however, this was a time when there always seemed to be too few colleagues with whom to share specific common interests, much less daily teaching loads. Although some resources were limited, a spirit of being engaged in novel and exciting activities continuously energized efforts, with success seemingly possible in just about anything undertaken. There was anticipation that a rapidly expanding interest in communication could help individuals and society in lots of ways.

2. Into the Academy at QIT

With a sense that all this seemed new for Australia, it was into this melee of opportunity and challenge that I found my way to QIT, to commence what became life-long interest in communication theory and practice. The second intake of students for the QIT course were expected when, with most academic staff still on summer break, I arrived to start work.

The influx of newly recruited academics in many areas of the institution meant that in company with a half dozen new colleagues from Business, a first "office" was in a screened-off area in a large room of an old Central Technical College building—the original "B block," just inside the front gate on the main driveway (pictured in this book's frontispiece). This office-cubicle contained a recently purchased desk and basic furniture of new design. It was located on the second floor of the building, with old double doors opening onto a distinctly unsafe-looking balcony overlooking the neighboring Botanic Gardens. This make-shift office in the "Tech" building was perhaps symbolic of the "on-the-run" reconfiguration of Australian higher education that was occurring.

Just graduated with an honors degree in English language and literature from nearby University of Queensland, personally this was a tremendously energizing time, experiencing a first full-time job to teach a range of communication subjects. The can-do approach of the leaders of the communication section and new colleagues at QIT offered a welcoming experience.

Research Interests

Largely through independent research, my own studies in communication had focused on aspects of language use in public communication, particularly in speeches and the mass media. Of special interest were effects embedded in language use through word and syntactic choice.

This built on understandings broadly outlined by George Orwell in his essay "Politics and the English Language"[24] and his "Principles of Newspeak."[25] It seemed a natural step, when exploring how language choice provided suggestive power beyond denotation, to link to observations about propaganda by the French philosopher Jacques Ellul.[26] Ellul was especially interesting for his explanations of how dogma is propagated to become powerful within a concurrently developed tribal culture. The popular and provocative insights of Orwell and Ellul were helpful to understand features of contemporary public communication.

Despite the disseminated insights and warnings that such thoughtful writers had provided about the propaganda from World War II, a new generation of ideological offspring of dangerous propagandists continued to hold sway within local politics and more widely. Ellul's perspectives offered valuable insights for both teaching and research–particularly his observations about the autonomic responses of human beings to memes, aphorism, or myths, which are sometimes expressed as incantations and become terms of reference for a tribal group.

Ellul had also described a powerful type of propaganda which was embedded in the presumptions of the social fabric. He suggested that messages consistent with this context could provide inner control over an individual–by a social force that deprives a person of individuality.[27] Such observations ignited enduring research interests and provided a framework for a range of research and writing pursuits over the years. From the outset, for study and teaching at QIT, it was of course routine to explore and take account of the insights of British, European, and North American academics and authors.

Teaching

QIT evolved its vision for teaching communication with a strong emphasis that communication was consequential to people's effectiveness interpersonally and professionally. A central teaching priority was to find ways to develop a student's curiosity, and thereby build significant abilities in communication within interpersonal, organizational, and social contexts.

Although these efforts were established mainly by Australian academics, whose own education was in traditional disciplines, each likely forged individual approaches by looking to a range of communication approaches and how these might help with teaching and research. The mix of British and European efforts in studies, teaching, and commentary were continuously strengthened. Significant emphases on cultural understandings and focus on semiotics, for example, were present in teaching at QIT from at least the early 1970s, but it was in the mid-to-late 1980s that QIT saw increased inputs from academics interested in semiotics and cultural studies.

From the outset, the academic staff in communication at QIT operated within a shared broad framework for communication study and teaching, and a generally cooperative goodwill pertained. Individuals recruited with a range of disciplinary and professional interests met the similarly wide-ranging teaching responsibilities. In the mid-1970s, communication staff were located for several years upstairs in the main administration building, "U block" (pictured on the front cover) and in "G block," during the planning and construction of a new

"B block," to house the Business School, within which the communication group was located.

My initial teaching responsibilities included subjects in writing, speech, and Australian studies, including some communication service areas. With five assigned teaching preparations each week, the priority was to deliver lectures, tutorials, and workshops well in these subject areas. Later teaching responsibilities included *Business and Society* and *Individual, Ideology and Society*. By the end of the second year, I had developed the new subject, *Professional Speech Writing*, and within a couple of years after this the new subjects, *Organizational Communication*, and *Communication in Politics*. These subjects helped to build students' understandings of communication in these contexts.

The teaching of speech writing, for example, focused on the qualities of speech presentation, based on principles and techniques of rhetorical stylistics. In one class exercise, to show how language choice projected the speaker's persona and personal style, students were asked to read excerpts of speeches distributed to them without the speakers' names identified. The students then described what personality characteristics they detected, along with how choices of words and syntax worked to deliver these styles, wrapping up with the inevitable guesses about the identity of each speaker.

Students were also asked to listen to and analyze the recorded speeches of a wide variety of capable speakers, to illustrate specific features of rhetoric and language style. The speakers studied included Sir Winston Churchill, John F. Kennedy, Martin Luther King Jr, Hitler, and Goebbels in text and audio or video recordings, and notable Australians such as Sir Robert Menzies, Dame Enid Lyons, Bob Hawke, Germaine Greer, Sir Roderick Carnegie, Justice Michael Kirby, and Gough Whitlam in text and an occasional audio recording, along with others involved in politics, business, and social advocacy.

The aim was to develop understanding of basic characteristics of persuasive language, calling on the rhetorical toolbox, stylistics, and other fields of language study. By the end of the classes, students applied their understandings to write a speech to be delivered by a "client" whom they found, afterwards critiquing their speech, the speaker, ethical considerations, and what they had learned. This was a fun and well received subject.

New Experiences

In addition to new professional experiences in the first year of teaching, new personal experiences included cultural and travel opportunities made possible by a regular paycheck. Just a few months into the new job, a newspaper advertisement indicated that Glenda Jackson was appearing in a production of the Ibsen play, *Hedda Gabler*, in Sydney. Remarkably, considering some inherited family assumptions about extravagance, I bought a ticket to the play and caught a flight south, for an overnight stay to attend the performance. Glenda Jackson was spectacular in the role. Before the performance, when mingling with other members of the audience in the theater's lobby, by sheer coincidence, I met a new colleague from the QIT communication program, Greg McCart, who with his wife had likewise decided to attend.

In the years ahead, local theater performances included seeing the celebrated Paul Scofield as Sir Thomas More in *A Man for All Seasons*, one of the infrequent local opportunities then to experience internationally celebrated actors. Attendance at another performance introduced me to a stunning local actress, Patsy McCarthy, in a fun production of *There's a Girl in My Soup*. As the best actors do, Patsy had command of the entire audience, with the ability through her eye contact to make each member of the audience sense she was speaking to each individually, even in the second row of the balcony.

After this performance, it was good to be able to help recruit Patsy from her successful speech and drama teaching practice to the faculty at QIT, where her strong presence contributed so much. Patsy brought a new level of excellence to teaching vocal delivery. She developed teaching programs in interpersonal and organizational communication, bringing insights from decades as an independent and highly regarded teacher of elocution and dramatic performance, along with deep experience in acting. Her celebrated performances included productions of both classic and popular plays. Among many accomplishments over the years at QIT was also Patsy's teaching a substantial number of students a quality of speech projection that enabled them to become some of the most exciting broadcast journalists in Australia.

Faculty Personalities

As academic groups tend to be, colleagues were a collection of personalities, each with different talents to bring to the education program. QIT attracted an interesting group of local and international characters. The leaders of both the institution and the communication section encouraged initiative, stimulating ongoing cooperative development of the communication program.

The academic staff appointed by 1975 were Phil Crowe (sociology), Jim Davies (writing), Tom Dixon (head of section, organizational communication), Val French (journalism), Peter Mayer (communication, media, and philosophy), Bruce Molloy (literature, history, and film), Joe Pinter (speech), and Jim Wrigley (business communication), as well as from the United States, Ken Gompertz (journalism), Keith Mabee (public relations), and Ward Welty (advertising). Other initial, new recruits were Greg McCart (drama and speech) and Napier Roffey-Mitchell (technical writing). Joining soon afterwards were Patricia McCarthy (speech and organizational communication) and Ridley Williams (audio-visual communication).

During the following years, recruited for new positions or to fill vacancies were John Burke (public relations), Pam Byde (sociology), Stan Fitzpatrick (advertising), Paul Gaskin (advertising), Len Granato (journalism), Vince Henderson (advertising), Chip Karmatz (public relations), Wayne Losano (department head, technical writing), Paul McLean (business and technical communication), Bernie Murchison (public relations), Jack Neate (advertising), Philip Neilsen (communication and literature), Roslyn Petelin (writing, speech, and organizational communication), Tony Stevenson (organizational communication), Graeme Turner (cultural studies), Tony Walsh (sociology), and Evelyn Wood (organizational communication).

Through team-teaching and friendship, I learned a great deal from a gregarious Canadian and fine teacher, Peter Mayer, who sadly died early in his life. On the morning before his classes, Peter was usually stationed at the photocopier, printing off copies of the day's newspaper articles that he had selected. He would distribute the news stories to that day's classes to stimulate student discussion, which he encouraged with his questions to challenge thinking. Peter taught subjects dealing with the roles of the media and business in society, as well as the relationship among the individual, ideology, and society. During his illness, he provided guidance to teach these subjects, which added yet another dimension to my thinking and teaching.

Ward Welty's family heritage included the novelist Eudora Welty, and he was previously an advertising copywriter at Tennessee Valley Authority. Ward's wife was from Alabama and made outstanding cornbread, which, combined with Ward's specially cut ribs barbecued in his secret sauce, made for many an awesome feast, until they decided to return to the United States.

Ridley Williams was an empowering colleague, who creatively led the development of audio-visual communication education and productions. He was largely responsible for leading the development of the facilities for television, film, the student radio station, as well as the substantial computing resources for journalism. On one occasion, with characteristic good sense, Ridley talked with me, and then intervened with the assigned consultant from the contracted fundraising firm, to adjust my role for the Institute's campaign launch that had me cast in a lead dramatic role, for which I had no training. Instead, at this special event in the Engineering foundry,[28] it was good once again to enjoy Patsy performing in partnership with another, each in leading roles that required their level of talent and training.

Teaching Writing

In these early QIT years, it was enjoyable to team-teach an introduction to writing class with Roslyn Petelin. As we met one day in my office, to work out how to deal with the writing deficiencies of bright students, who had little grasp of grammar, a series of phone calls from our mutual colleagues interrupted us. Without any mention of the callers' names being made, after about the fourth or fifth call, Roslyn wrote down the names of each of the callers. Her finely attuned voice teaching talents enabled her to recognize how unwittingly my speech tone and pace changed to mirror a caller. Over many years of collaboration with Roslyn, it was energizing to work with her to improve teaching programs and conduct courses for industry and government advancing the teaching of writing.

In common with colleagues throughout the English-speaking world, we annually welcomed students into the communication degree, for whom the teaching of grammar from about the 1960s to the 1990s was denied in prior schooling. Many were bright but could not write at all well. When the students arrived, they held in one hand high entry scores and, in the other hand, a collection of concerns, delusions, and anxieties about what writing would be expected of them in tertiary education and employment. Comments they shared in small group discussions, after being introduced to what writing would be expected at QIT, included:

> Primary school was where I received 90% of what I know about spelling and grammar.
>
> Throughout my school life I've had very little actual teaching of the rules [of grammar]–it's been more application which we're expected to know already but frankly don't.
>
> I hope that my lack of grammatical understanding can be amended and that my total ignorance of computers likewise rectified.
>
> I feel inadequate in spelling and structuring sentences.
>
> In primary school, grammar was studied mainly. However, in high school essay writing took over.[29]

Students had some analyzing, synthesizing, and evaluative abilities. Soon enough Roslyn and I redesigned the first week's writing class to provide just a few introductory remarks, followed by a grammar diagnostic test to help identify the common grammatical difficulties, along with seeking thoughts about writing. Although most students had serious gaps in basic knowledge of conventional English usage, most wanted to improve their knowledge. Every semester, we agonized over the wasted energy and emotions caused by the misinformation about writing that many students had gathered through their schooling. Students were frustrated and tired of the contradictions that different levels of education and different teachers presented as "the way to write."

The students' future employers were united in what they expected of graduates:

> 100% accuracy in dealing with the verbal context.

Developed ability to establish and maintain professional and personal relations.

Immediate grasp of the professional and personal environment.[30]

By implementing a reader-based, problem-solving approach to writing, significant improvements were accomplished relatively quickly. The guidance and rigor provided in this writing course was vital for the students' futures.

Roslyn went on to become an authority on problem-solving approaches for writing, computer-based writing, and publishing. She later moved to a faculty position at The University of Queensland and developed a stellar international reputation through her books, writing for publication courses, conference and industry presentations, and MOOCs—courses of study made available over the Internet without charge to a very large number of people, which, to date, have allowed about a million students to benefit from her teaching worldwide. Through two and a half decades, she edited the *Australian Journal of Communication*, to make it an excellent publication. In her tremendous efforts to sustain and enhance the journal, she received great support from David McKie, as well as from Leila Green, Judy Motion, and Shirley Leitch.

Australian Teaching Needs

Up to the mid-80s, there were few textbooks or published Australian case studies useful for teaching and research. As mentioned earlier, students expressed a bias against American texts and, to a lesser extent, against the few early British publications. Some of us compiled booklets with Australian materials for use in class. Australian academics progressively developed textbooks and studies of communication with Australian context.

Another challenge that presented was to transition from teaching writing with manual typewriters to teaching students to write using computers. Computers were just coming into workplace use, and neither the communication teachers nor the administrative staff at QIT had computers. During the late 1970s, apart from a relatively few communication academics doing quantitative studies, the common experience with computers was to watch accounting, science, and engineering academics carrying their boxes of punch-cards across campus to the institution's central sorting machine, located in the printing center.

It was a media relations professional at Bell Labs in Murray Hill, New Jersey who alerted me to an enlarged role of computers in writing, during a visit there in late 1979. He demonstrated a version of the *Unix Writer's Workbench* program, available then only on a mainframe. With this introduction, it was possible on return to Brisbane to get on-line via a local university computer, by placing a telephone handset in a modem cradle, for access to the software on a Bell Labs computer in the United States—early days indeed.

Journalists in Australia were soon transitioning to key their stories directly into computerized compositors for typesetting. Partly to ensure journalism students would have computer proficiency for writing, the first-year writing subject that Roslyn and I taught moved quickly to teaching writing on computers. During a break between semesters, the Apple IIe computers purchased for the student teaching laboratories disappeared into faculty offices, so that we could learn how to use them before the students arrived for classes.

Later, a successful grant to develop a prototype *Writer's Tone Editor*,[31] as an early computerized tool to analyze writing style, provided an Apple Macintosh and printer. The Apple Education Foundation provided the equipment and a partnership with John Gough, the Head of Computing Science, delivered the coding needed in Modula-2 to complete the grant.

QIT Strength

Much strength of the QIT communication program came from complementary initiatives in teaching, research, and community service. QIT actively encouraged academic staff to undertake applied research and consultancy activity with the community. The institutional mission of bringing theory into practice for the benefit of the community helped inform the teaching and research.

Academic staff delivered presentations or workshops for academic, professional, and industry audiences, conducted research, and wrote for publication, while developing courses for both the teaching program and for the continuing education of employees in commerce and government. During thirteen years as an academic, a personal aim was to contribute in each of these areas, and the opportunities abounded.

When Tom Dixon later became deputy to the director of the institution, he expanded this community interchange more vigorously institution wide. The senior management of QIT advocated that:

> These activities play a vital role in the lives of academic staff as they help to sustain authoritative teaching and assist in maintaining and developing close links with industry. They have undoubted economic benefits to the state and the nation.[32]

As Tom led the Communication Section when I arrived at QIT, the formative stage of this approach was already in place.

Community Interaction

One week after arriving at QIT, I received an invitation from a colleague, Jim Wrigley, to join him on an externally funded consulting project. The brief was to recommend marketing communication options and to develop the communication materials for a proposed mail order insurance package, for the State's association of fruit and vegetable growers. Jim designed the project and arranged for an experienced marketing lecturer, Reg Hardman, to lead the effort. Then, it was into "the deep end," driving with Reg onto fruit and vegetable farmers' properties in nearby Redland Bay, to sample potential customers' interests through surveys and conversational interviews.

This was the first of many varied consulting assignments encouraged for the next two decades. Consulting projects approved under the Institute's consulting policies provided a real-world laboratory to help strengthen academic work. Some early projects required travel to Sydney to teach railway station staff how to make clear public announcements amid the noisy railway station platforms, to Rockhampton to teach public address to a political party's candidates, along with a wide range of projects in various locations over time–all opportunities to make a difference to the understanding and practice of communication. The encouragement of community interaction stimulated efforts to help establish the Society of Business Communicators (Queensland), which resulted in my serving two terms as president.

Ongoing were conference presentations and articles for various academic, industry, and community audiences, including The Royal Society of Queensland, service clubs such as Rotary and Toastmasters, or community activists such as Friends of the Australian Broadcasting Commission. Community contributions for six years also included writing monthly columns on communication and management topics in the Confederation of Industry's *Enterprise* and the Chamber of Commerce's *Voice of Business* publications for members, while being a correspondent for *The Australian Environment Management Review*.

Continuing education programs were provided for accountants, advertisers, auditors, communication professionals, engineers, fundraising professionals, managers, personnel consultants, managers of quality control, school and college principals, surveyors, industry training professionals, and other groups.

Experienced Leaders

The encouragement of academics to be in contact with practitioners and organizational leaders brought into the classroom the wisdom and experience of people with significant accomplishment in communication. A national leader, met in 1980, was Mr. Justice Michael Kirby. He was then Chairman of the Australian Law Reform Commission, and went on to serve from 1996 to 2009 as a Justice of the High Court of Australia. At a congress of *The Australian and New Zealand Association for the Advancement of Science*, he chaired the Communication: Access and Privacy session, in which I presented a paper. As a particularly astute speaker, Michael willingly discussed his approach to public speaking. We later met at his office in Sydney, for an interesting and valuable discussion that provided insights about this distinguished Australian's approach to speech-making. During the conversation, he continuously requested his assistant to bring a variety of speeches into the office, to share specific insights and thoughts. He showed great competence handling a wide range of speech settings, with a developed ability to use humor in creatively engaging ways.

Another dynamic professional met early in the QIT years was the author and political speechwriter, Graham Freudenberg. At a workshop on advanced speech writing that I organized at QIT, Graham generously shared experiences and thoughts with a group of graduates from the *Professional Speech Writing* class and other practitioners.[33] He also gave insight to the heady days of his working with then prime minister Gough Whitlam. After sending to Whitlam my stylistic analysis of a speech he had delivered in 1971 in parliament, Whitlam wrote in thanks and responded to a point about his likening the Liberals to the Bourbons. He clarified his precise purpose in the speech was to make clear that the Liberals, like the Bourbons, had "learnt nothing and forgotten nothing."[34]

For a field trip I organized for QIT students to visit with advertising and communication professionals in Sydney, Graham kindly opened the door to New South Wales Premier Neville Wran's communication folks. Sometime later, when in Sydney to present a conference paper, after phoning Graham at short notice, he suggested meeting the next day at the restaurant in the Wentworth Hotel. For a journalist turned political operative, who worked late into the night, this was to be at 11 am for breakfast of omelet and champagne, accompanied by much interesting conversation, and finishing up late in the afternoon.

Leadership Accountability

A variety of other involvements in seminars and conferences provided opportunity to get to know many talented and outstanding people in areas of professional practice, one of whom was Malcolm Duce at the *Institute of Internal Auditors of Queensland*. In the State of Queensland and beyond, he helped to change the face of how government, corporate, and nonprofit organizations used annual reports. With the support of his wife Halina, Malcolm initiated a transformation of the annual reporting function of organizations, so that the annual report became more truly a measure of performance.

Through Malcolm's driving force to lead the *Institute of Internal Auditors' Public Sector Awards* in Queensland and through involvement in the *Australasian Reporting Awards*, he annually saw to every element of the report judging process, to ensure the success of these programs. From 1981 to 2006, Malcolm's tireless attention to improve the quality of the annual reporting of government, business, and nonprofit organizations resulted in 1,176 submissions to Queensland's annual awards. It was substantially his enthusiasm and follow-through that ensured the visible improvement to 19 times the number of awards for excellence in 2006 compared with the inaugural year of the awards, with a total of 197 awards of excellence through these years.

Malcolm championed communication as a key component of the Award criteria and made the annual reporting process meaningful and useful for stakeholders. He directly advised communication professionals who compiled the reports and their senior management, as well as empowering the adjudication panel as mentors. His efforts elevated the awards as accountability for organizational leaders. It was both a pleasure and an honor to serve on his adjudication panels in Queensland from 1986 to 1996, for many years as master of ceremonies at the Presentation Ceremony in the Parliamentary Annex. As Malcolm nicely put it, this took "the Awards back to where they belong—with the politicians at Parliament."[35] At Malcolm's invitation later, he enabled my coordinating the adjudication of online annual report awards from the United States for the *Australasian Reporting Awards* for several years.

Early Students

Students in the QIT communication degree courses had a range of interests. Many were very bright, mostly attracted to doing something useful in society with their communication ability. Others, who were also bright, had missed out on entry to their first preference choice of a medicine or dentistry course, and had named communication as an assured second option for entry to a tertiary education degree course. Students found that during the three years of study for a Bachelor of Business, both the course and the industry developed rapidly.

The teaching at QIT was enjoyable, if demanding at times, with the students resourceful, mostly focused on study to find a satisfying career path. They were generally diligent, with few requesting extensions for assignments. The oddest excuse for not submitting an assignment on time was from a student who came to the office with his sister, after one Easter long weekend. Perhaps a characteristically Aussie story, which his sister came along to corroborate, was that the two of them were hitch-hiking several hundred miles north, to visit their parents for the long weekend, when the utility truck they were riding in the back of suddenly turned off the highway, to speed west into the bush.

Apparently, many miles after they had yelled enough and broken the back window of the driver's cabin, the vehicle finally stopped, so that brother and sister jumped from the truck and ran away as fast as possible. They then faced a long walk back along an unpopulated road to the main highway north, eventually finishing their journey and spending much of the long weekend helping with the police investigation of the incident. On the Tuesday morning following, when the assignment was due, they came to my office prepared with names, phone contacts, and personnel numbers of the police constables involved in the follow-up investigation—of course, they secured an extension on the assignment.

On another occasion, late one afternoon three young blokes, who turned out to be later-year students, arrived at my office and unfolded from an ice box a large parcel in aluminum foil, as a gift. Inside were freshwater barramundi fillets from their weekend catch in far North Queensland, more than 1,200 miles / 1,900 km away. They said they had caught too many fish to eat themselves and wanted to share their good luck. They described also how only two of them fished at any time, the other member of the group charged to sit nearby on the riverbank with a rifle, just in case of crocodiles.

Student Careers

At the completion of the communication degree, students navigated a variety of careers, many in new job roles, in government, nonprofit organizations, and corporations. They were employed by public relations firms and government departments as managers or officers responsible for public relations or information, by advertising agencies and retailers as media managers, account executives, researchers, and copywriters, and by print and electronic regional and metropolitan news organizations as journalists, sub-editors, and editors.

Some secured senior positions, such as chief executive of a small computing firm, executive director of a convention bureau, women's editor of a major metropolitan daily, national public affairs managers of major mining or retail companies, advertising manager for a retail chain, and others within nonprofits and government. Each new placement produced a sense of breaking new ground for academic staff just about as much as for the graduates. Almost all had to develop approaches to communication without existing models or in-house mentors to forge new approaches—the graduates were pioneers in many areas.

Entrepreneurial Leaders

Two students from the first group to enroll in the course illustrate different leadership careers developed in corporations. As a student, one had found a way to focus nearly every assignment, including for sociology, on various aspects of a major international fast-food corporation. At the end of his final year of studies at QIT, I had a chance meeting with this student one cold January afternoon in the Florsheim shoe store on Union Square in San Francisco. As part of the education that he arranged for himself beyond the QIT course, he had just completed study units with the corporation's "university" in the United States. He was on his way to Lake Tahoe for some winter skiing. When visiting with this graduate years later at his successful fast-food franchise, located between Brisbane and the Gold Coast, he was exploring negotiation of a second franchise.

Another savvy graduate became chief executive for the South-East Asia region and then president of a restaurant chain within the parent corporation, based in Los Angeles. He initially expanded the corporation's outlets throughout

Australia and South-East Asia. With this success, he was called on to tackle a challenge in the United States operations of franchise-holders nearing retirement age being unwilling to spend the necessary funds to modernize their restaurants. Since a restaurant customer's experience of furnishings, décor, and service was part of the fast-food product, this was causing a continuing decline in customers. After meeting individually with franchise-holders nationwide, he had to dissolve the franchise structure, sell-off the company restaurants, and oversee that company's bankruptcy. He then returned to Australia and further expanded franchises and the parent corporation's facilities throughout South-East Asia.

During one of his times in Australia, when I managed the QIT Communication Centre, he commissioned a contract to solve a customer queuing problem that resulted from the popularity of the restaurants in Australia. They were so popular that, when potential customers saw the long lines of people waiting outside, they kept driving to a competitor. Academics in mathematics, who had developed mathematical models to solve telephone queuing challenges on busy telephone switchboards, were able to identify key blockages to the flow of seating diners more rapidly, through to the busing of tables afterwards. As a graduate of a combined communication and marketing course, who had received a mathematics prize as a student, he quickly saw potential solutions. Whenever visiting his office, just before our meetings his senior managers would emerge through the meeting room door carrying large blocks of computer printouts, but he never seemed to have paper in his hands. Quick mathematical abilities, along with interpersonal and marketing savvy, put him well ahead of many others.

Such abilities and creative approaches to think about communication challenges in organizations or society were representative of the inventiveness and persistence of many of the students, who graduated into different areas of communication practice. They continuously drew on qualities that were integral to their success within the creative approach of the education program.

3. National Professional Developments

From the mid-1970s, via academic gatherings and relatively few Australian publications, teachers and researchers progressively learned more about the communication courses or research of colleagues across the nation. Diverse efforts under the broadly accepted banner of interpersonal and mass communication were evolving.

These included studies of communication networks, channels, processes, or effects. Some researchers focused on information diffusion, agenda-setting, or uses and gratification approaches. Other efforts provided a variety of textual, semiotic, readability, or content analyses, to examine message types in verbal, visual, or personal nonverbal communication, including discourse analyses seeking to identify embedded ideology. Many studies focused on a particular communication object, such as a conversation, film, letter, interview, speech, or television program. The analyses tended to be rooted primarily in the perspective or methods of an analyst's academic discipline, such as linguistics, literary studies, semiotics, speech and drama, psychology, sociology, economics, politics, or history. At this time, obviously neither the Internet nor social media other than the telephone existed

Conferences on Communication

Some conferences attracted nationwide attendance, showcasing analyses, reports, and interpretations of research or teaching approaches. Featured at these conferences, as well as in smaller specialist events, were panel discussions or streams of papers focused on hot topics or issues. Recurring topics often related to public or corporate policy, such as to probe the influence of mass media or technologies on audiences or on society. Frequently these included analyses of media ownership, news bias, children's television (including television as electronic baby-sitter or potential educator), television as entertainment or cultural phenomenon, sexism in advertising, and television violence. Other focus areas included political communication broadly and election campaigns, the politics of information, freedom of information, technologies of communication, or telecommunications, to list just some.

Specialist events or seminars were also held to explore concerns within communication applications in business, technical, and science contexts, or within professional fields of public relations, journalism, advertising, broadcasting, film, television, or speech and theater. A great benefit of such a smorgasbord were the interesting insights within so many offerings.

In the academic institutions where teaching and research under the banner of communication occurred, the focus was on human communication, with little or no attention to communication in animals, cells, or mechanical devices—areas that were being explored in variously named university or polytechnic/college departments concerned with psychology, biology, or the technologies.

Polysemic "Communication"

Within study, teaching, and practice, "communication" was polysemic, and no one had a map of the growing variety of interests. In the academy, some described their efforts as contributing to a communication discipline, while others saw efforts as less coherent, preferring to characterize communication as a field with many disciplinary interests. Perhaps the best descriptor for this variety was what elsewhere were called:

> ... "assemblages" [of interest] not automatically coherent, not readily theorizable, and requir[ing] work for... maintenance... [with] searching for the unifying principles... likely to be misleading or counterproductive.[36]

When reviewing the dynamic of what was loosely called a communication studies field, in Germany, North America, and other places, Robyn Penman has noted[37] that there was a lack of consensus on subject matter, arising from the heterogeneous academic backgrounds of its scholars,[38] which left communication as a contentious and divided field.[39] This somewhat pertained in Australia, due partly to the heterogeneity of the individual academic backgrounds or interests. Perhaps, as the social scientist Craig Calhoun points out:

> Communication is one of the fields least likely ever to be defined by a common method... [with] ...great diversity in methods of doing communication... [and] ...great diversity in methods for studying communication...[40]

Calhoun's view was informed from his perspective that research, especially in North America, had remained "split between the embrace of scientific universalism and humanistic focus on contexts and cases."[41] But if, as he later notes, "part of the work of theory in any field is to help integrate its disparate parts and lines of inquiry,"[42] the decade or so from the mid-1970s in Australia seemed not to be a time in conferences or publications of getting much beyond the disciplinary or application home-base or "bower" that most concerned a teacher or researcher.

This was especially ironic, given that the concern was communication, a word with semantic relations in the Latin to *communicare*, suggesting "to impart, participate, share" and *communis* suggesting "joint-common."[43]

Shared Focus

At QIT in the mid-1970s, regardless of any differing priorities and concerns about emphases among academics involved in research, or teaching, or in areas of professional practice, a focus for teaching efforts was found. Common understandings developed, not through isolated pursuits, but by working together to deliver a coherent program for the benefit of the students.

A shared purpose in this academic group was to develop communication understandings, to enhance the abilities of students and practicing professionals in a wide range of applications, "from speech to writing, to filming, broadcasting, and so on."[44] Contributions to different aspects of the teaching program also benefited from the input of practicing professionals.

With an aim to build linkages between academics and practitioners, I sought articles in mid-1976 to launch a journal, *Australian Scan*.[45] Reflecting the scope of a speech communication association I had founded, the journal was concerned with "Public Address, Organisational Communication, Interpersonal and Small Group Communication, Creative and Educational Drama, Television, Radio and Film." At this time also, with a similar aim of bridging the academy and practice, a colleague Val French produced a new publication, *Inter Connections*,[46] published in 1976-7 for several issues. Val's students undertook as class exercises the initial design of both publications, with *Australian Scan* later becoming the *Australian Journal of Communication*.

Production of the Journal

A quick look back to the early years of producing the journal shows how much publication technologies and production methods have changed. The first six issues of the journal were typeset on an IBM strike-on compositor (which had a similar appearance and function as the IBM Selectric Typewriter). This was located on the desk of the Assistant to the QIT Registrar, who would find time to type copy between other work. This was the only typesetting equipment in the organization. Editing the journal then required cutting and pasting paper printouts of copy, using lots of liquid "wite-out," and laying out the offprints as time permitted, usually on the dining table at home at night and on weekends. Production, printing, and mailing costs were met through initial subscriptions solicited from institutional libraries in Australia and overseas, and few individual subscribers (initially, for two issues annually, $5.50 local and $8 overseas).

The communication courses taught then in colleges of advanced education, institutes of technology, and universities ranged from the art of speech in the British tradition, to interpersonal and group communication, to media studies and mass communication, to business and technical communication more in the North American tradition. Research and thoughtful commentary focused on interpersonal and mass communication from the wide array of disciplinary perspectives and areas of application. This was the context for my seeking articles suitable to publish in *Australian Scan*. Initially, the journal was a slim volume in which communication teachers, researchers, and practitioners were encouraged to share information and explore enhanced understandings of human communication. During the 1980s, the journal increased in size, range, and reach, aiming to reflect the tremendous changes and growth of communication as an area of study and teaching in Australia.

The editorial position of the journal was to publish the most thoughtful studies and insights from among the articles submitted. A peer review process was introduced, and the journal was able to sustain publication at a rate of two issues per year, with subscriptions as the only financial support. Most importantly, in the early 1980s when the *Australian Communication Association*—now ANZCA—was formed, with members mainly in the academic institutions, the Association adopted the journal as a membership benefit, which not only added subscriptions but also progressively increased the potential for seeking an even more diverse range of articles of interest to this growing group.[47]

In 1982, the journal was renamed *Australian Journal of Communication* and, following my move to an administrative role in 1987, I confidently bequeathed editorial responsibility to Roslyn Petelin, who strengthened the publication for 25 more years. In response to her request for perspective on the original motivation for the journal, to be included in her final editorial in 2013, I noted that:

> A persistent reason was to help stimulate and encourage substantive interaction and to serve as a vehicle to help improve understanding among colleagues who were drawn from diverse disciplines to communication studies. As a young faculty member, I wanted to encourage more boundary-spanning studies, better mutual understanding, and rigorous enquiry to help advance communication research and teaching in Australia.[48]

Conference on Interpersonal and Mass Communication

It was with this spirit that a week or so after publishing the first issue of the journal, in December 1976, I traveled to Sydney to present my first conference paper at a national conference, at New South Wales Institute of Technology (NSWIT)–now University of Technology Sydney. The conference was held at the Broadway campus, within a new but ominous prefabricated concrete tower of a building, typical of the architectural monstrosities that, worldwide, somehow manage to insinuate like triffids to blight higher education campuses.

The conference attendees were gathering at a time when Australia was flavored with what felt like a pioneering spirit to advance communication education, in which anything seemed possible and energy levels were high. What was quickly apparent to a first-time conference attendee was that many attendees knew each other from previous interactions. There were distinct groupings of people, who were interested in either interpersonal or mass communication, and relatively few involved in the teaching or research of both.

The conference papers dealt with a broad range of communication topics. Interpersonal studies were concerned with teaching, drama, and small group interaction, as well as diverse interests in political and intercultural communication. At least as wide interests were evident within approaches to mass media and mass communication study and teaching. Afterwards, the conference organizers managed to group the papers under these broad headings, for publication of the conference proceedings.[49]

"Invisible College?"

One conference paper from John Galloway, then at Macquarie University, reported on the potential for "invisible colleges" in Australian communication studies. He analyzed a survey of 63 of the 145 attendees external to the host institution, who completed the survey just prior to attending.[50] He suggested that communication was perceived by people involved in communication study and teaching in Australia to be very much an interdisciplinary concern. His study suggested psychology, English, education, and sociology were considered the four leading disciplines. Respondents also perceived mass communication as the most important unit of interest, and television led the way in terms of various other interest categories.[51]

His paper is an interesting snapshot of one group of national conference attendees. The registered affiliations of attendees were roughly, 47% college of advanced education/institute of technology (or 34%, if attendees from the NSWIT host were not included), 21% technical college, 21% university, 7% unknown, and 4% government/industry. Present at the conference were some already well-known educationalists in mass media, mass communication, and film, such as Ina Bertrand (La Trobe University), Patricia Edgar (La Trobe University), and Jerzy Toeplitz (Australian Film and Television School).

Galloway projected the concept of a "prestigious" group within the field, which he called a potential invisible college of shared contacts. Eleven of the seventeen attendees comprising this group had key linking roles, cutting across the broad group structure.[52] What emerged also was that one person appeared to be the major linking agent among the diverse clusters of individuals, who were otherwise mainly preoccupied within their own cluster. It was speculated that this might be Professor Henry Mayer, who was at The University of Sydney, with expressed interests in political theory and the politics of information.

That he was considered the major linking agent was perhaps because many academics and quite a few practitioners had received one or more of Mayer's prolific notes that he sent to people to stimulate interaction—at that time, by sending and receiving through the "snail mail" (no email yet) brief, scribbled or typed notes, alerts, and suggestions on some clipping or other item of interest. Soon afterwards many of these notes or observations would appear in the long list of "media briefs" in his publication *Media Information Australia*, first published in 1976. Mayer was in daily contact with a huge number of individuals in the field, prior to the conveniences of the Internet and email. He was forcefully living a catalytic role in information dissemination to provoke thoughtful inquiry.

Although Galloway was appropriately cautious about generalizations when interpreting from the small sample, he concluded:

> Although most of our respondents are located in various groups largely along institutional lines, it appears that most are linked to each other indirectly through a small prestigious group who have high levels of contact between each other across institutional boundaries.
>
> Communication is perceived by people in communication to be very much an interdisciplinary concern.
>
> It seems that the invisible college to some extent may embody the norms of what is regarded as important in the field.[53]

He acknowledged that it was difficult to say just how influential was the invisible college that he tentatively projected, other than noting that it appeared to be operating as a medium for contact and interaction between people who were otherwise separated geographically, and with diverse viewpoints about the nature of their professional field.

What was clear were subsets of some aligned interests within interpersonal and within mass communication. Presentations and workshops at the conference assumed very different paradigms and approaches for study, teaching, and practice. Perspectives on communication also diverged according to attendees' ideologies, which was very evident in the different approaches and conceptual frameworks in a variety of interpretations about ethical considerations.

Proposed Association

There was some discussion at the closing session of the conference about forming an association for academics with interest in communication, with a plenary session recommending this—as noted in the proceedings, resolving to "discuss the formation of a professional association for tertiary scholars and teachers of communication." Perhaps largely because of the breadth of attendee interests and perspectives, any overall coherence for alignment was not readily evident. Although a communication students' group got it together to form an association at this conference, despite many conversations among the academics in meetings and over coffee and excellent international restaurant offerings, their teachers did not.

During the conference, I shared copies of the just-off-the-press first issue of *Australian Scan* and encouraged individuals to submit articles for consideration for the next issue. This was prior to "publish or perish" impulses that later bubbled up in the academy. Nonetheless, a trickle of contributions arrived early in the new year for the second issue of the journal, including the articles published from W.J. Crocker, Frederic A. Gruber, John J. Galloway, and J.E. Baxter. Published in the subsequent issue for 1977, was another article solicited from P.D. Marchant, then head of the school of humanities and social sciences at NSWIT, examining the 1975 Australian federal election and the press. Subsequently, I had contact with only a couple of other academics at that institution.

Broadening Interests

Soon after the conference at NSWIT, in late December 1976, I traveled for the first time overseas to attend in San Francisco the conference of the largest and oldest communication association in the United States—the *Speech Communication Association,* established in 1915. During conversations with conference attendees, including former presidents of this Association, and some leading faculty in the field, there was much interest in the communication education developments in Australia. From these discussions, some recommendations for possible addition to the QIT course included specific topics for advanced level students, such as organizational communication and campaign speechmaking.

My research interests also developed through conversations and research at the Rhetoric Department of the University of California Berkeley. And an intriguing discussion resulted from a call to Stanford University's "communication group" when seeking an appointment with an appropriate faculty member.

Martin Esslin, the authority on the theater of the absurd who had coined this term, had just returned to serve as professor of drama. He graciously welcomed a visit, the duration of which stretched as he probed my interest in propaganda. Esslin shared insights about his work after 1943, when he had participated in counter-propaganda radio broadcasts. This was for a British propaganda broadcaster during World War II that pretended to be a radio station of the German military broadcasting network. Its broadcasts were in German, since the Nazis required people in occupied countries to listen only to radio broadcasts in German. Immediately after Hitler's speeches were broadcast, Esslin and others would provide analyses of the speeches that were unfavorable to the Germans.

Ever since this discussion, I wondered how much the time Esslin spent in this activity impacted his later describing the theater of the absurd. During our conversation, he urged a shift of my Master of Arts research to focus on the radio station's files, which he believed were still untouched at the BBC archives—and he was prepared to facilitate access for a study that he felt could be groundbreaking. It was intriguing and wonderful advice that could have defined a different personal future.

Discussions with both faculty and practitioners, at the Sydney and San Francisco conferences and beyond, pointed to the value of sustaining a broad-based scope for the journal.

Scope of the Journal

In the second issue of the journal, in June 1977, its continuing scope specified interest in interdisciplinary or specialist articles on:

- Public communication
- Creative and educational literature, speech, drama, film, and television
- Organizational communication
- Interpersonal and small group interaction
- Intercultural communication
- Mass communication and media studies.

This list was prominently positioned in the front of the publication, with the intention of encouraging a robust range of articles "to promote study, criticism, research, teaching, and application of communication principles."[54]

Through subsequent issues, articles were also solicited to focus on specific areas of communication interest, including politics, interpersonal communication, nonverbal communication, and the media, with book reviews and brief notes also introduced. With the aim of progressively reflecting the broad range of interests in communication teaching and research in Australia, the journal published both solicited and unsolicited articles.

The subtitle of the first two issues of the journal suggested concern with "speech communication." As noted in the editorial of this second issue though, "speech" was considered to have "wide scope... interpreted to describe all human communication..." Articles published in this issue dealt with implications in linguistics and linguistic philosophy for communication understandings, public explanation of economic matters, the limits of a "persuasion viewpoint" and advantages of "agreement/accuracy" to judge what communication works, the operations and marketing benefits of a speakers' bureau, QIT's professional speech writing subject, and recommendations for improving oral and written communication among management, employees, and customers.

Included also in this 1977 issue of the journal was an article from Bill Crocker, providing an historical survey of speech teaching in Australia. He noted an attempt in 1970 to form a national association of speech-communication-interested individuals and reminded that the conference at NSWIT had "decided to found a national organization and elected a committee."[55] This suggestion was to be pursued more than two years after the NSWIT, December 1976 conference.

Developing Communication Initiatives

During 1976-9 throughout Australia, the concentrations of teaching or research in communication took on more definition across a widening range. These offered students what appeared to be a wider variety of roles in journalism, film, television, and a host of professional communication areas. Ongoing developments in communication education reaffirmed the appropriateness of emphasizing a broad scope for the journal, including by an adjustment in the journal's subtitle to human communication for the December 1977 issue.

In early 1978, Harry Irwin submitted an article to the journal tracing the development of communication subjects in the Bachelor of Business degree program at Kuring-gai College of Advanced Education (now part of University of Technology Sydney). The goal of these efforts was to provide both professional and personal development, with learning activities sequenced to increase learner experience and learner accomplishment.[56]

This represented a consciously cross-disciplinary approach. It went beyond the largely pragmatic and genre-bound constraints of many of the communication service subjects in operation for so many years in institutes of technology and colleges of advanced education. This was a broadly conceived effort to integrate theories for effective learning about interpersonal communication.

QIT Communication Grows

The QIT communication program also evolved further during 1976-9. Tom Dixon navigated the addition of a journalism and media strand to the degree. Ridley Williams developed both the curriculum and facilities for audio-visual communication and Bruce Molloy energized the development of film studies.

The total of 16 academic staff consisted of Dixon, Molloy, Crowe, Wrigley, Davies, French, McCarthy, Mayer, Pinter, Roffey-Mitchell, Williams, and me continuing, now joined by John Burke, Paul Gaskin, Paul McLean, and Tony Walsh, as well as support staff and a large group of part-time teachers.

As communication section head, Tom had developed the teaching program while he was completing a second master's degree, in linguistics. Following some structural reorganization within the institution, the communication section became a department within the School of Business, necessitating advertisement for the head of department position, which *de facto* Tom had done well for a decade. The institution decided to appoint a PhD from the United States to head the department from 1977. Tom was granted special leave to undertake a PhD program in organizational communication at Rensselaer Polytechnic Institute, in upstate New York.

Later, the new head of department supported an initiative I was exploring to organize class teaching into less than three days a week, to commute to Sydney weekly to also teach part-time at a Sydney institution. He felt this would expand research and consulting opportunities. With a fuel crisis in Australia at the time, and concerns about whether the planes could keep flying, however, the responsible institutional manager in Sydney got cold feet and nothing further came of the suggestion. By the time Tom returned, with his PhD completed, the head of communication department position was vacant, and he successfully competed for the role.

Armidale Conference

It was during early 1979 that notice was received at QIT that Bill Crocker was convening a conference on oral communication competence in children—to be held in Armidale in northern New South Wales, in June 1979.

An issue of the journal was already in production that incorporated a mix of articles about writing, interpersonal communication, and mass media (number 6, June-November 1979). And a double issue on nonverbal communication (numbers 7 & 8, December 1979-November 1980) was scheduled to follow, with the articles for this issue in the hands of a guest editor from the United States. A subsequent double issue of the journal was in the planning stages, to reflect broad interests of communication teaching and research.

Just prior to leaving for Armidale, Crocker phoned to ask me, as editor of the journal, to chair a meeting at the conference to establish an Australian association of individuals committed to human communication. I took a flight to Armidale, for the first time on a six-seater plane, in an almost cloudless clear blue sky. During the final approach to the country airport, a serious air pocket made all passengers grateful for seatbelts fastened and, even more grateful, when landed, to step onto firm ground.

The conference theme was "Developing Oral Communication Competence in Children," attracting about 60 attendees mainly from around Australia. The attendees were teachers in teachers' colleges and high schools, others involved in the government oversight of curricula, a few academics in teacher education from Australian universities, and seven invited United States speakers with accompanying significant others. Mostly, attendees were interested in children's language development.[57]

Even so, when some of this group met to discuss the formation of a national association of human communication lecturers, quite diverse backgrounds and interests within the specialist focus of the conference became more apparent. The range of interests included English, speech, drama, linguistics, psychology, art, curriculum, and educational assessment. Perhaps unsurprisingly with this variety of interests, during an extended discussion, the options to focus the association ranged widely.

But come together we did finally, to agree a collective interest in establishing the *Australian Communication Association*. An organizing conference was proposed for the next year to inaugurate the Association, and this was to be held in May at the Raywood Conference Centre, in the hills near Adelaide, South Australia.

Prior to that organizing conference, from November 1979 through January 1980, I visited with leading mass communication researchers in London, Leeds, Leicester, and the Glasgow Media Group, as well as with communication faculty and practitioners in New York and San Francisco. These conversations again highlighted a value for the journal to seek to represent sufficiently the widest possible, important developments in communication research, teaching, and practice.

4: Communication Meaning

At the inaugural conference of the *Australian Communication Association* in May 1980, a small group of enthusiastic teachers, mainly from colleges of advanced education, assembled to shape the organization. Participants included Bill Crocker from Armidale College of Advanced Education (now part of University of New England), with some wider interests in interpersonal communication, psychology, and business communication addressed by Harry Irwin, Bill Ticehurst, and Paul March from Kuring-gai College of Advanced Education, Grant Noble from University of New England, and Jim Baxter from Swinburne Institute of Technology (now Swinburne University of Technology). Summaries of four papers that were presented were included in the *Australian Communication Association Newsletter*, June 1980.[58]

With a hope that the new Association might progressively enable purposeful, broad-based initiatives for research and teaching efforts, I offered a brief discussion paper on "Finding Communication Meaning in Australia," commencing with the quote from Nicholas Garnham that:

> Communication studies is not a discipline. It is not even a coherent field of study. It is an illusion based upon the poly-semic nature of the word communication...[59]

If "communication studies," as it was much talked about, was to develop as a field, it seemed advisable to be clear about ambiguities surrounding use of the word communication, in the academy and in everyday conversation. At least six major groups of meanings and senses were apparent in the use of the word by teachers and researchers, namely:

- Field (C_F)
- Application (C_A)
- Message Types (C_M)
- Object (C_O)
- Subject (C_S)
- Process (C_P)

These were outlined in Figure 1 of my discussion paper:

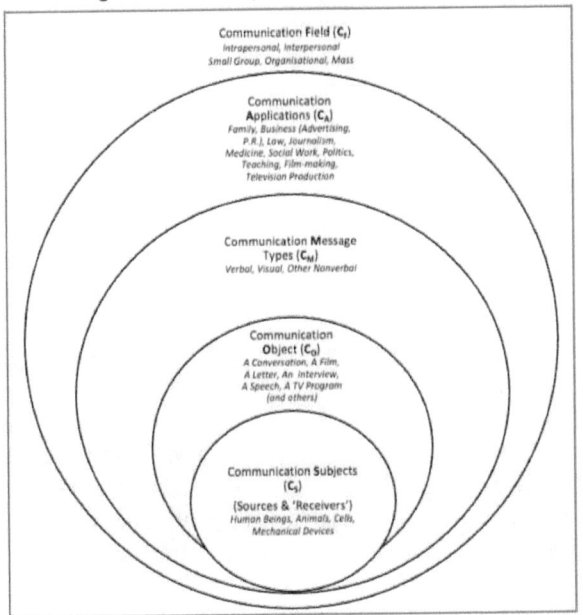

Figure 1: Studies in (Human) Communication

Perhaps the formation of the Association would provide opportunity to purposefully explore some of these different meanings and implications within studies and applications, potentially enabling anyone involved in teaching and research to see a "map" of sorts–to clarify where each of us was pursuing interests relative to the rich array of others' interests.

This seemed necessary if a purpose of the Association might be to help develop such a loosely described field as "communication studies"–even if only for researchers, teachers, and practitioners to better find a common basis for discussion. In Australia, the areas of study in communication were still young enough to reap the benefit of such mutual understandings and potential for cooperation and mutual inclusiveness.

Some of the concerns I suggested to consider at the conference, were that:

1. Mass media and mass communication teachers and researchers, who were not truly represented at the conference, effectively studied two types of communication (human and technological), and therefore had special contributions to make to the new Association–especially since the technologies of mass communication were likely to be increasingly important in everyday life. It also seemed that researchers of cellular, animal, and mechanical communication (C_s) could contribute to human communication study. Psychologists studying the social ethology of

animals informed human nonverbal communication, such as the research of my former psychology teacher at The University of Queensland, Professor Glen McBride. Studies of this type were popularized during the previous decade by publications like Desmond Morris's best seller, *The Naked Ape*.

2. The Association's purpose might embrace a broad concern with "communication" study, perhaps outlining a range of interest areas, with suggestions for planned complementarity in exploring some of the senses identified in Figure 1.
3. The Association and its members might particularly focus on furthering the study of:
   3.1 The most specialized aspects of the communication <u>process</u> (C_P), with an aspiration that from these studies real theoretical knowledge would flow. Which posed the question, where are the communication theorists in this country? (Professor Henry Mayer's comment at ANZAAS 1980 was that there were none.)
   3.2 What value might come from examining core concepts and principles in different studies across the <u>field</u> of communication (C_F)–so that, say, the concept of "gatekeeping" from mass communication research might be explored for its potential to enhance and be enhanced by understandings from interpersonal research.
   3.3 How we might be able to link principles developed by scholars from the different disciplines or approaches used to study communication.
   3.4 Any commonalities that can be shared about the teaching or research of communication principles, as these are applied in different areas of practice, such as business, law, nursing, politics, education, the family, and so on.

In the early stage of development of the Association, it seemed 3.3 above was particularly important, since the many scholars then studying communication rarely included more than a passing nod to approaches taken by others. A related important challenge for the Association to face seemed to be whether a cohesive approach to communication might be developed to provide value to communication teachers trained in established disciplines.

A key question was whether we might avoid traveling again the path of some North American sociological or psychological approaches to communication (C_F), which might not much consider philosophical or broader ideological consequences of communication (C_O). Another concern potentially worth the Association's attention seemed to be to address the fragmentation in the study of communication because of two trends:

1. Using different "meanings" (or "definitions") of communication that often marked out narrow interest areas (in any of C_F, C_A, C_O, C_M, C_S, C_P,: any of which emphasized different conceptual considerations) and
2. The transfer of a narrow focus on "communication" from a particular disciplinary or other limited viewpoint across a range of communication research.

Whether communication was to become a discipline, I left for others to consider following on from the discussions at that year's congress of the *Australian and New Zealand Association for the Advancement of Science*.[60] But if "communication studies" was to develop as a field in which researchers, teachers, and practitioners could find a common basis for discussion, it was suggested the two trends noted above might be offset by:

- Conscious cooperation between academics from diverse disciplines to seek strong bridges, rather than to inadvertently dig chasms between and among researchers, teachers, and practitioners involved in communication. As a matter of policy, the Association might consider subsidizing or otherwise encouraging interdisciplinary communication research.
- Encouragement of communication researchers to seek better understanding of diverse theoretical explanations of communication.

When I had visited with Professor Jay G. Blumler at University of Leeds during the previous year, he vigorously advocated similar needs in relation to concerns about studies in mass communication. He had urged cross-disciplinary initiatives as potential remedies: (1) exploratory studies from an initial common standpoint, such as sociology, to provide perspective on the interface of social organization and mass media organizations; (2) consideration of conducting media content studies to bring together disciplines of semantics, semiology, and English to analyze culture; as well as (3) pursuing psychological and allied perspectives to consider processes of audience consumption, utilization, perception, response, and effects.[61]

An analogue of some such approach for the study of the broad field of communication in the Australian academy might have borne fruit. Australian teachers and researchers seemed at the time to have avoided the full inheritance of the muddy concept of communication that Frank Dance and subsequent researchers in the United States were still seeking to clarify. Dance had identified fifteen conceptual components in communication (C_F):

Symbols/Verbal/Speech
Understanding
Interaction/Relationship/Social Process

Reduction of Uncertainty
Process
Transfer/Transmission/Interchange
Linking/Binding
Commonality
Channel/Carrier/Means/Route
Implicating Memories
Discriminative Response/Behaviour Modifying Response
Stimuli
Intentional
Time/Situation
Power

Also, I suggested for consideration exploring the eclectic approach that Stephen Littlejohn had outlined.[62] If pursued in Australia, this might have been a starting point to develop better understandings of communication ($C_{P,F,A,O,M,S}$), with intentional consideration of the contributions that different theories and perspectives provide to the conception of communication.

It seemed inadequate simply to jump on a single theoretical "hobby horse" and ride it home–although that option was certainly available. Frequently enough, we had seen teaching modules and even entire subjects that tended to treat McLuhan, Klapper, Shannon and Weaver, or Barthes, with little or no correlation with other perspectives and not much other context-setting.

If the focus for study was to be communication, it seemed important to find a common language,[63] a common purpose, and a united willingness to recognize and accommodate a wide range of concerns of people studying and teaching under the banner of "communication." Otherwise, the likely alternative could be a conglomerate of fragmentation-causing, limited perspectives, or isolated communication study upon study, each of which might remain hostage to the home-ground of the original discipline of a teacher or researcher, in English, politics, education, speech, rhetoric, sociology, or psychology, and so on.

A potential vision for the new Association could be to help develop some common ground. This was likely only if the Association members, and particularly its executive, as its most frequent spokespersons, advocated communication as a multifaceted and dynamic process, while stimulating a range of synthesizing explanations and theoretical perspectives that captured insights from intentionally, broadly informed approaches to analysis.

With communication itself polysemic, at the very least, a pluralistic understanding of communication, derived from a variety of study approaches, seemed important to advance study and teaching, as much as for practice. This might have offset a concern at the time that self-styled communication consultants would ride their own "hobby horses" into areas of practice, before seriously identifying their purposes and the contribution that more than just one aspect or approach in the growing field of communication understandings could make.

If isolated or idiosyncratic activities were to occur unrelated or unchecked, perhaps it would not be long before the businesspeople, the nurses, the educators, the administrators, and other practitioners might turn on, or tune out the teachers and researchers in communication, dissatisfied with platitudes or conflicting perspectives on communication.

Comparison with Canada

In Canada in the early 1980s, some faculty there were also addressing clarifications of communication terminology. The editor of the *Canadian Journal of Communication* and its predecessor *Media Probe*, Earle Beattie, indicated this when he noted my paper from the Raywood conference.[64] The development of the communication field in Canada around this same time had some glancing similarity to what occurred in Australia.[65] But in other areas than speech, such as journalism and mass communication, the Canadian developments had occurred as early as 1945, with programs established at Carleton University and the University of Western Ontario. Many more efforts were established from about 1965 onwards.

The roots for the Canadian developments were found widely, in sociology, psychology, political science, philosophy, economics, political economy, another social science, or in the humanities. But rhetorical studies in Canada emerged strongly early, with some input from United States scholars. In contrast in Australia, rhetorical study was offered in schools and universities within the study of classics subjects until the early twentieth century.[66] But a fully developed degree-level education program in expression and communication, which included study in rhetoric, did not seem to be available until around 1970. This was within the English department's honors program in language and literature at The University of Queensland–where former QIT colleague, Roslyn Petelin, later developed a writing, editing, and publishing course.

The main similarity of the Canadian developments to the evolution of communication education in Australia seemed to be that the interest of educators in communication originated from a wide variety of disciplines.

Commonly in Canada, the teaching of professionals in journalism and studies of mass communication occurred separately from programs in other areas of communication.[67] Interestingly, Henry Mayer had contact with the then editor of Canada's *Media Probe*, Earle Beattie, from at least 1976, when Mayer launched *Media Information Australia*. In a letter to Beattie, Mayer noted:

> Thanks for Media Probe which is much livelier than many more pretentious mags, I have put you on the list for MIA 1, which ought to be out this month.

I depend for resources re typing and printing on others who are less keen than I am. I fear that our local stuff—which is not intended to be probing, like yours, though I would much prefer this—will bore you to tears, But we'll see. Prof. Henry Mayer The University of Sydney, Australia[68]

Further Evolution of Journal

As mentioned earlier, just prior to the inaugural conference to organize the *Australian Communication Association* of May 1980, an issue of the journal was well along in its development, *Australian Scan: Journal of Human Communication* (numbers 9 & 10, December 1980-November 1981), the final issue using this title. This issue was to include survey articles that I solicited, on semiotics (David Sless), linguistics and communication studies (Gunther Kress), interpersonal communication (Harry Irwin and Joseph MacDoniels), organizational communication (Tom Dixon), communication networks (John Galloway), and mass media studies (Henry Mayer). These survey articles were published alongside articles on cable television, interpersonal communication, communication competence, communication apprehension, ideological unity of discourse, and an article on ruling class ideology in Australian Soap Opera. Also, Grant Noble, who was now associate editor of the journal, had suggested a target paper approach, offering for criticism an article that he had written with Elizabeth Noble on Foreign News in New South Wales. Henry Mayer and Andrew Bear provided perspective in commentaries on this article. In addition, the issue included an index of all articles published in the journal to that date.

Going forward, the journal was renamed *Australian Journal of Communication* (numbers 1 & 2, January-December 1982),[69] to better reflect the range of interests of members of the young Association. Articles by Glen Lewis and by Robert Hodge offered thoughtful mediations of some growing dichotomies. But there seemed little appetite for a unifying vision for communication theory.

Connectors and Commentators

Mayer assumed a growing importance not only as a connector of people and ideas in relation to mass communication and media industry developments, but many engaged in the field also appreciated his broader-ranging syntheses and insights about communication research. He knew more than most about research and practitioner initiatives, and he welcomed, stimulated, or otherwise encouraged a range of efforts. He knew what he knew and was able to quickly grasp the essential concepts in studies, whether already familiar or new to him. He was respected and could go to core assumptions with constructive critiques. Mayer became a substantial interpersonal force advancing some better mutual understandings.

During conferences, Grant Noble, especially via his questions about or critiques of papers, also quietly listened and contributed to conversations, encouraging consideration of differing perspectives or, where appropriate, the convergence of thoughts. For the journal, Grant similarly offered both helpful ideas and support. His research traversed a range of concerns about psychological considerations in communication, including children's interaction with television, teenagers' uses and gratification with television, international studies of television flows and media usage, Indigenous peoples' self-image in the mass media, why people feel compelled to answer the phone, and attitudes toward technology as predictors of use. He was to be much missed when he died too soon. Grant's thoughtful insight and encouragement through his interactions at communication conferences, in his book reviews and critiques of articles, as well as through his own studies, provided substantive value.

Beyond these voices, also notable were David Sless, from 1975, and Robyn Penman, on her return from Britain in 1980. Each pursued fresh approaches to information and communication theory and applications. Initially, Sless was at Flinders University, then became the Foundation Chairman of Standards Australia's Committee on Signs and Symbols in 1976. In 1985, he established the Communication Research Institute in Canberra. He sustained multiple contracts for government form redesign, based on his insights in learning and visual communication. At national conferences especially, Sless challenged assumptions within semiotic perspectives. He put attention on how signs are interpreted and probed assumptions in broader perspectives of communication, vigorously evaluating core principles.

Penman illuminated communication as a collaborative undertaking that developed new understandings and new knowledge. She would later describe an encompassing approach to communication theory. The critiques and publications by Penman and Sless strongly countered earlier instrumental and transactional views of communication. Each spoke with a strong ethos of sustained independent thinking, informed by psychology, philosophy, and more broadly. They opined from positions of being separate from the established teaching and research institutions, and their efforts were distinct in how they placed communication in its societal and cultural context.

In 1981 at Kuring-gai College of Advanced Education, Harry Irwin and Elizabeth More convened the first broadly-based conference of the *Australian Communication Association*, opening the conference with an important observation that it "would be unfortunate for Australian communication scholars to become totally preoccupied with the struggle between contending epistemologies and methodologies."[70] Soon afterwards in the conference, Bill Bonney argued critically for sociological and ideological interpretations of communication.[71] Other approaches were explored in this and later gatherings of the Association.

National conferences were also convened in 1983 by Russ McKinnon and T.J. Larkin from Warrnambool, on organizational communication, and Graeme Osborne, Robyn Penman, and David Sless from Canberra, on communication in government and politics. These and other conferences included some academics from the United States or Britain. In addition to such gatherings, academics at QIT continued to benefit from ongoing regular interactions with colleagues internationally, including through faculty recruited over the years from the United Sates (Gompertz, Granato, Karmatz, Losano, Mabee, Walsh, and Welty), and colleagues who had studied there (Crowe, Dixon, Stevenson, and Williams).

Broadening Awareness

With the aim of stimulating further interaction in a wide range of study and teaching efforts, for the 1983 issue of the journal (number 3, January-June), additional survey articles I solicited were on interpersonal communication (Harry Irwin), semiotics (David Sless), language (Stephen Muecke), mass media (Henry Mayer), and organizational communication (Russ McKinnon). Together with a survey of communication studies in the subsequent issue (Gunther Kress), these articles provided some overview updates. Particularly the articles of Irwin, Sless, and Mayer provided snapshots of how broad Australian communication teaching and research efforts were—especially when compared with the interpretation of speech communication that seemed to be advocated as the initial focus for the national Association, just a few years earlier at the 1980 Raywood conference.

Debate on perspectives of communication continued in the journal's pages and at the Association conferences. And many voices were important in shaping thinking about both broader and more specialist aspects of communication, including Andrew Bear (on television violence and multicultural broadcasting), Warwick Blood (on media models, agenda-setting, and political communication), John Fiske (on television culture), John Galloway (on information networks), Gunther Kress (on linguistics, discourse, and cultural studies), Elizabeth More (on telecommunications and organizational communication), Virginia Nightingale (on understanding media audiences), and Graeme Turner (on cultural studies), to name just some.

An interesting exchange in the journal in 1985 centered on Irwin's article that revisited interpersonal communication competence, with a rejoinder from Penman, outlining the case for what she suggested as a more truly relational model, as well as a further response from Irwin.[72] But wide interdisciplinary and boundary-spanning studies did not take root during my involvement with the Association up to 1987, when I took on a new role in QIT's administration.

Roslyn Petelin sustained editorship of the journal from 1988, when I passed its production to her care. For 25 years following, she published a variety of perspectives cheek by jowl in the journal, stimulated interactions, and sustained an upward trajectory on the quality of intellectual discussions, including some collaborative speculations and initiatives. For the next half decade and beyond, Henry Mayer, Grant Noble, Harry Irwin, and David Sless, with additional commentaries by Roslyn Petelin and Robyn Penman, made many contributions to help clarify concepts and assess potential for some congruence within the communication field.

QIT School of Communication

During the early to mid-1980s, the QIT facilities for teaching were substantially enhanced, adding quality television/sound studios and upgraded computerized facilities for journalism teaching. The students produced radio news programs for broadcast, as well as a wide range of creative projects. The graduating students annually showcased final-year presentations, which attracted attendance from the campus, industry, and the community.

From 1986, drawing on Tony Stevenson's years in public relations practice, the School established a consulting and research center, for which I became the inaugural manager. Tony also helped to strengthen a perspective on communication as seeking mutual understanding. By 1988, the QIT department had become a School of Communication with a total of 20 academic staff.[73]

Course Expansions

QIT course offerings expanded during these years well beyond the undergraduate degree with its early professional strands of advertising, journalism, and public relations. A master's degree in Business Communication through coursework and dissertation was available from 1985. In 1988 a two-year graduate diploma in communication practice was offered, which included professional strands in advertising, audio-visual communication, journalism, public relations, organizational communication, and later, fundraising communication. The graduate diploma enabled part-time completion of a communication credential in any of the professional areas, which attracted students seeking new careers in communication–including an increasing number of graduates transitioning from other occupations, such as teaching. Later a professional doctoral degree in communication was made available.

The idea for the fundraising strand originated from a discussion between Bruce Molloy and a member of the QIT governing council, Betty Byrne Henderson[74] about the prospect of the federal government not continuing to fully fund tertiary institutions. Bruce suggested that an educational program for fundraising professionals would likely be needed to fill that funding void and others like it, and Betty agreed to back the program.[75] She provided funding to conduct a seminar on philanthropy at QIT, led by the director of the Fund Raising School, Hank Rosso, who was transitioning this private school to become part of the Center on Philanthropy at Indiana University.

Her funding also enabled input for the development of the graduate diploma through a visit of Professor Robert F. Carbone, located at the University of Maryland. An accomplished local fundraising professional, Everald Compton, provided further input as a visiting faculty member. During this time, I had a hand in the continued development of the graduate diploma course, while also marketing and teaching a range of professional education courses in fundraising for QUT, and as an adjunct faculty member of Indiana University's Fund Raising School.

Though no longer working as an academic staff member from late 1987, it was a communication framework that I applied to responsibilities for the institutional advancement efforts of the university and beyond.

Catch-up

After catching up a bit on some more recent writings on communication in Australia and New Zealand, it seemed earlier dichotomies concerning communication theory may have found some accommodations. One perspective that seemed promising to help evolve an encompassing theory of communication was outlined in an article in 2012, unsurprisingly, by Robyn Penman, "On Taking Communication Seriously."[76] Penman suggested reconstruction of communication theory around "communication viewed as a process of joint action between active agents who, in their engagement, generate new understandings and knowledge."[77]

Such an approach, in the way that she outlines, is consistent with but more developed than what Tony Stevenson sought to bring to QUT in the early 1980s from his studies at University of Hawaii, which were influenced by the East-West Center. Penman suggests that investigating communication needs "some agreements... about a sense of communication that allows us to talk about it, research it and teach it in such a way that distinguishes it from other human phenomena."[78]

Important to Penman's proposition is Agency, as "the capacity of people to use their will to initiate joint action and to continue to act jointly within the process."[79] She advocates the tripartite themes of intersubjectivity, agency, and praxis as needed to "...form the foundations for a communication discipline... readily applicable to mediated as non-mediated contexts."[80] As Penman and/or others continue to extend and execute on these thoughts, it will also be key, as she indicates, to appreciate that a practical theory is

a) concerned with everyday communication practices,

b) provides an evolving grammar for talking about those practices,

c) generates a family of methods for exploring situated communication practices that

d) evolve out of the interaction between participants in those practices (including the "researchers"),

e) changing both the practice and potentially the methods as they proceed, and

f) are assessed by their consequences—specifically in terms of how it makes human social life better.[81]

Anyone who believes communication matters in serious ways[82] should benefit from taking up her challenge. Penman's articulation, in my opinion, is important and ought to be welcomed as a framework worth exploring and extending. Researchers of discourse pragmatics or rhetorical stylistics, for example, have long focused on some of these concerns. For what it is worth, almost a half century of my own intentional use of communication understandings, to secure results internally and externally for organizations, sits well with the approach she proposes. As Penman suggests, finding shared "grammar" and methods between a variety of studies and social or psychological analyses, or both, would likely enrich all these areas of inquiry.

Pathway Forward

Hopefully, some such approach will continue to be developed and pursued vigorously. Perhaps this might be revisited by the *Australian and New Zealand Communication Association* (ANZCA). After more than four decades since its founding, and regardless of recent practical challenges, the Association still advances important efforts. Teachers and researchers who care about communication are pursuing new work in key areas, including digital communications—sharing perspectives and raising awareness of the depth of research into communication and media studies in Australia and New Zealand.

5. Doing It

More than a decade of external relations activities from the mid-70s had helped to shape my understanding of ways to apply communication in practice. Consulting, training courses for industry, and applied research projects within Australia and internationally provided insight into a range of corporate, government, and nonprofit organizations.

Brushes with politics in the early 1980s added experiences, through directing a successful but difficult campaign to re-elect a local alderman, helping to develop and publicize policy initiatives of a branch of a political party, standing for election as a political candidate, and serving on the advisory or governing boards of government and community organizations. These were quick immersions in the backrooms of politics, requiring focused interactions with a variety of politicians and volunteers.

Communicating Strategically?

When I asked a leading politician whether his party's parliamentarians might coordinate their communications strategically, he'd looked thoughtful. Then he pointed to a fountain pen in my shirt pocket, replying enigmatically that politicians had their own brand to promote, just like the company interested in promoting its own pen. That observation highlighted an ongoing challenge for the communications of political parties in many countries. In the local politics then, that perspective became one of the major challenges that proved devastating to that party.

Among the many people met at this time, it was a volunteer campaign director, a local resident John Matthews, who stands out. John had business and political savvy, as well as a talent to see strengths in people and situations. His ability to creatively organize successful actions from what others saw as a disorganized morass was inspirational.

During a first campaign meeting, while others opined their gripes and fears, John would write himself a list of "to do's" on the back of whatever piece of paper was nearby. Then for 60 to 90 minutes, he guided the conversation and checked off, for each "to do," who was now committed to doing what by when—so that when the meeting closed everyone felt good about what was accomplished—a rare talent to ensure focus on what mattered. When I was asked to stand as a political candidate soon afterwards, John was a strong supporter and guide at a time when the party and parliamentary leadership made poor decisions that led to its annihilation in the election.

Candidate Campaign

This crazy campaign was conducted for almost a year alongside QIT teaching and other professional efforts—which required some juggling. On one occasion during a three-day period, the intersection of campaign and academic responsibilities meant flying from Brisbane to Melbourne to present an academic conference paper on organizational communication, then, back to Brisbane for a breakfast fundraising event the next morning for my campaign, followed the same day by getting back on a plane to Canberra to present a conference paper on political communication, then returning to Brisbane the following day.

One of the local politicians who attended the fundraising breakfast and supported my efforts in other ways was a local alderman, who was a progressive thinker with a background in journalism. She had an intuitive and professional competence handling the media. Additionally, during a walk through a busy shopping area in the electorate in support of my campaign, she greeted and reached personally to almost every passer-by or shopkeeper on both sides of the street. She was an accomplished and well-known retail politician, who would soon become Lord Mayor.

Tasks as a candidate included waking early each morning to check and replace any campaign posters around the electorate that were removed overnight (then part of urban politics), or to attend breakfast political meetings or events, on the way to a full workday of lectures and other tasks as a faculty member. After classes finished at 5 pm or 9 pm, most nights included more political activities until 10 or 11 p.m. or later. Door-knocking the electorate, along with shopping center and other community activities to meet residents of the electorate, occurred mainly on weekends at first.

As one of many local candidates, competition for media coverage was stiff. Attention-getting gimmicks secured some mentions in the metropolitan press, like the suggestion of a colleague, Chip Karmatz, to include in the mailed invitations to a campaign gathering a balloon that carried the message, "Hot Issues, not Hot Air." Another time, a campaign volunteer's biplane flew at 500 feet (150 m) along the river corridor, which was about level with one of the City's tallest buildings at the time. Above the venue where the Prime Minister was launching my opponent's campaign, the biplane circled, dragging a long, printed message that was critical of their policies. This the local press called a "high flying attack" message, as the plane circled for over an hour.

In collaboration with communication graduates who volunteered for the campaign, we developed a media profile in the suburban press and on local radio, to get attention to some substantive community needs. In the final six weeks before the election, which was classified as the official campaign, the law required taking vacation leave from QIT, since the institution strictly speaking was a government organization.

Although it was energizing as a political candidate to be able to develop and offer initiatives to try to make people's lives better, it was not to be. Among the many post-mortem letters from party leaders, was the astute comment from a vice president of the party executive, referring to the party's historic decimation in the election:

> We might have hoped for a better result—but when the tide is running so strongly against you, and you have a split raft it is impossible to advance, no matter how hard you paddle.

That summed up much, for all the efforts of many. As QIT responsibilities grew, active involvement in politics had to diminish. Afterwards Tom Dixon, now the deputy director of QIT, in his understated way commented about my political involvement that this was good experience.

Bridge to Practice

But it was the transition from research and teaching to administrative roles at QIT that most shaped opportunities to bridge communication theory and practice. My external relations efforts for the institution increased when appointed in 1986 as the inaugural manager of a consulting and research center within the School of Communication.[83] This role also involved participation to support the efforts of QIT's comprehensive fundraising campaign—the first undertaking of its kind in an Australian tertiary education institution.

In early 1987, when talking with the on-site fundraising consultant, who was about to complete a four-month assignment, the director of QIT, Dennis Gibson, came out of his office nearby. He asked the consultant how much of the one-million-dollar, three-year campaign goal was raised. After determining details of what was in the bank, confirmed in writing, and what were verbal pledges, Dennis turned and said to me, "I would like you over here next week." Next day, in the office of his deputy, Tom Dixon, with my head of school, Bruce Molloy, and then again with Dennis, a secondment was negotiated to a part-time role, to coordinate the follow-up of pledges and to complete the campaign.

This fundraising campaign was early among the many changes soon to reshape the structure and funding of higher education in Australia. From 1851, when The University of Sydney was established as the first university in the colonies, Australian universities inherited academic structures and traditions largely from Britain. The Federal Government funded higher education, and the states administered the institutions. In 1987, a single private university was established, named for its founder, British-born Alan Bond—who in 1983 had secured international fame for mounting the Australian bid to break finally the New York Yacht Club's 132-year dominance of the America's Cup yacht race.[84]

In 1988, major changes to higher education in Australia were introduced by Labor's Federal Minister for Education, John Dawkins.[85] These included partial privatization measures, such as the reintroduction of fees for domestic students and a requirement for universities to become more entrepreneurial. To meet these requirements, some institutions soon looked to the outreach approaches of universities in the United States, especially to raise funds.

Changed Role

In late 1987, after accepting the full-time role to lead QIT's fundraising and alumni relations efforts,[86] a message of welcome arrived from the QIT Director, who was at Harvard for a residential course for university presidents. He wrote encouragingly that this move from academics to fundraising, for Australian higher education would be akin to the scale of change experienced by the engineers who moved into computing at an earlier time.

The role required stepping outside the academic field of communication, to become familiar with ideas and insights of academics throughout the institution. The role took shape as a broker-communicator, applying communication understandings to translate some complex, jargon-filled but exciting teaching or research ideas in a wide variety of areas.

By asking academics to imagine what would accelerate their efforts at the highest level of excellence, a lead academic in a specific area would draft as "expert witness" a statement of aim, benefits, outputs, process, and budget. Ordinarily after some redrafting, these succinct "project statements" reflected the excitement and promise, identifying the benefits of an initiative to a potential funder, the institution, and the community. In the spirit of Theodore Roosevelt's urging to keep eyes on the stars and feet on the ground, it was possible to craft a variety of initiatives with potential for funding. Much like a good resume, a project statement became the guide for conversations with a potential funder, to explore any match of interests.

No roadmap and little intel were available to guide this effort, other than feedback on the draft project statements from some business and community leaders, who had volunteered to serve as an external advisory group. This group assessed the potential of projects and, where possible, made connections with potential funders. During an initial visit, the project statement was usually kept in a back pocket, during an oral presentation to corporate, government, or community leaders of influence and means. Frequent follow-up was needed to refine alignment. Positive results from these outreach efforts resulted often enough in substantial funding to benefit the education and research programs.

Improving Education Resources

QIT academic staff in engineering, the sciences, information technology, information security, business, law, and, after an institutional merger, the arts and education, were at the forefront of study and teaching in a wide range of endeavors. The research efforts included invitro-fertilization of fish and aqua-farming, cybersecurity, forensic electronics in audio-taping criminals, electron microscope forensics, cancer treatment, orthopedic and ophthalmic research, even the handling of telephone queuing on busy switchboards mentioned earlier, as well as a host of other areas. It was an Aladdin's cave of initiatives.

The private funds raised enabled new courses, research, student support, and academic appointments. It was satisfying that the fundraising efforts helped to provide some educational opportunities that were not previously available. Despite our location in the largely non-head-office city of Brisbane, within which we initially confined our reach, it proved possible to attract some substantial funding. And, despite the stock market crash in October 1987, by the end of the following year, QIT ruled off the campaign as completed and over goal, a year earlier than the campaign's original target date.

Changing Culture

Throughout these actions, it was essential to respect everyone's egos, as well as to function within the still evolving rules for private funding in an institution under state government governance. Australia's culture and history presumed in most participants' minds that public taxes were to pay for education, which made for some "interesting times" when implementing this new approach.

Some academics took readily to partnering for the visits to external organizational leaders. And some areas of study or teaching had more potential for finding a funding match. But a "private shop" attitude among academics predominated then, along with some harboring of an ideological opposition to entrepreneurial activity, so deeply felt in areas of the academy. Quite often academic staff or deans and heads of school would politely meet. Initially, it was mainly QUT's leader, the chancellor, some governing board members, and the QUT Foundation president who were involved in the successful fundraising, delivering additional funds to academic use.

Faculty leaders also exhibited varying levels of responsibility and responsiveness in expending the raised funds, sometimes only reluctantly seeing to the agreed use of the private funds. Progressively, through the engagement of faculty leaders who provided role models, including Professors John Corderoy, Malcolm Cope, and Miles Moody, the returns from academic-partnered fundraising gradually improved.

On-the-Job Learning

Key to completing the campaign a year ahead of the original target date though was the energy, drive, and talent of Bill Blair, the volunteer president of the recently created QIT Foundation. As chief executive of the conglomerate QUF (Queensland United Foods), he somehow found time, for many months, to set appointments with his wide network of contacts—for visits we made together to business leaders whom he knew, at times at a pace of four to six visits a day, for two to three days a week.

These visits were particularly helpful to complete the campaign successfully, but also Bill was a character, who liked to share a lot about business, networking, and enjoying life. More than once, when arriving at the reception desk of a major accountancy or law firm or another company, in a serious voice, he would say that he was there to conduct an audit. Without giving his own name, he would ask for the CEO by name, and issue instructions not to touch any papers. Frequently, the message would come through to "show Mr. Blair in," or the CEO being visited would arrive at the front desk, rarely surprised to see Bill, tipped off by the style of his announcement.

He started professional life as a research scientist at the Australian Government's CSIRO (Commonwealth Scientific Industry Research Organisation). As he told the story, he grew tired of working long hours for the low wages of a researcher and moved into marketing. There he still worked long hours but was paid enough, as he told it, to take home flowers and champagne.

Later, Bill became marketing manager for Warner Lambert, based in Canada with responsibility for pharmaceutical marketing in the Americas and other parts of the globe. After some years of even longer hours and countless international flights, he said that when he came home late one night from Japan, his wife convinced him to return to Australia. Soon afterwards, Bill secured a role leading the expansion of QUF for the supply of a wide variety of consumer foods in Australia and internationally. He also grew the original business to virtually monopolize milk supply in eastern Australia. He was a thorough leader, and organizationally savvy.

Decade of Funding Growth

Through continuous collaborations, the annual income to the institution's Foundation increased for ten years. In 1989, with the transition of QIT to

Queensland University of Technology (QUT), a successful special purpose campaign funded new applied research efforts. This campaign funded professors, who were to lead research in information security, quality, maintenance engineering, building management, and other areas.

The top leadership of the institution understood more than other university leaders in Australia at the time about some of the essentials for fundraising success. The institution's leader, his deputy, and successive chairs of the governing board/chancellors, Vic Pullar and Cherrell Hirst, along with some influential board members got it, in terms of the heft and help they were positioned to use. This was an early lesson in how to make outreach with the collaboration of volunteer business and community leaders, which proved helpful in later roles.

Indiana-Purdue University Courses

Toward the end of the second year of fundraising, QUT supported my travel to San Francisco, to attend a one-week course of The Fund Raising School that Hank Rosso had established. This course and another week visiting with the Advancement Division at Rensselaer Polytechnic Institute in Albany, New York, provided a working understanding of some best practices for fundraising and alumni relations. These two weeks of immersion in principles and practice provided the overview and detail to continuously make improvements to QUT's fundraising strategy and practices.

Continuing contact with Kay Sprinkel Grace, a lead teacher from the San Francisco fundraising course, helped tremendously to integrate professional vision with practical understandings. Valuable collaborations with practitioners in North America and Great Britain also provided insights to progressively adapt and apply at QUT. Ongoing contact led to attendance at further courses and becoming an adjunct faculty member of The Fund Raising School, by then located within the Center on Philanthropy at Indiana University.[83] This resulted in my marketing and teaching the QUT/Fund Raising School courses for eight years throughout Australia and New Zealand.

A mix of communication consulting, teaching, and the development role itself enabled acquaintance with some of the most thoughtful and energizing business, government, and nonprofit leaders in the region. Overseas professional travels included Canada, Europe, Malaysia, New Zealand, Singapore, United Kingdom, and United States. In many technology areas, Australia's commercial and research initiatives were expanding exponentially, and this provided welcome opportunity for some of the innovative partnerships developed with industry.

Professional Service

Other professional activities included serving on the governing board of the professional body, The Fundraising Institute of Australia, which involved leading the introduction of the nationwide examination and accreditation of fundraising professionals, CFRE (Certified Fund Raising Executive). This required approval of the applicability of the United States CFRE program by both fellow members of the Australian fundraising professional body's national governing board as well as the United States professional body's agreement to expand their national system for the first time internationally, to Australia. While there was much general goodwill toward this initiative, many preconceptions and objections had to be settled about concerns and details, which in Australia were partly stimulated by a touch of cultural suspicion of things American.

Forging international agreements can be slow and, at other times, surprisingly quick. On one occasion, on a trip from Australia to Washington DC to finalize the CFRE agreement, which thankfully was also for other business, it was a long wait outside the meeting room of the responsible committee of the United States organization, as they dealt with pressing domestic matters. When finally permitted to enter the meeting room, the committee chair and members enthusiastically expressed eagerness to enjoy what was left of the early spring day among the Washington DC sunshine and cherry blossoms. The committee chair then granted about fifteen minutes, including questions, to explain and advocate Australia's adoption of the U.S. system of CFRE accreditation. Fortunately, with some rethinking of what were the "very key" issues to address, this was enough.

Along with other members of the Australian organization's governing board, we all sat the United States examination, and were awarded the certification of CFRE.[88] To address some objections from the Australian governing board members, I rewrote portions of the United States examination and chaired the inaugural National Accreditation Board. When the smooth running of the Australian system could be assured, it was good to bequeath the continuing operations to fellow board member, Nigel Harris, who had the essential qualities of being both honest and highly competent.

New for Australia

In 1991, the new alumni organization of QUT responded positively to my proposal to establish the QUT Outstanding Alumni Awards to recognize the accomplishments of graduates in the Arts, Built Environment, Business, Education, Health, Information Technology, Law, and Science.

This initiative was satisfying for its focus on the real accomplishments of a talented group of people. It helped to direct the graduates' attention to an additional opportunity for their continued interaction with the university over a lifetime. Though a well-established expectation in North America, this was a major change for Australian higher education. The event to present the awards grew quickly, thanks to the efforts of talented development staff, and had to be moved off campus, initially to the Heritage Hotel ballroom.

As income results and more areas of outreach increased, the staffing of the development office could gradually grow. Recruiting colleagues with the sophistication to interact with corporate and community leaders and with academic staff proved most successful by employing QUT communication graduates who had some professional experience.

Lacking Australian peers in university fundraising at the time, it became routine for the continued development of QUT's efforts, to continuously reach out internationally to leaders of advancement efforts and faculty who had experience of high-performance operations. This included designing benchmarking projects to partner with quality advancement efforts in North American and British universities. Related initiatives included creating a benchmarking conference in San Francisco, to help accelerate the professional development of QUT development staff, through their interaction with professionals from McGill University and Strathclyde University. These activities led to my arranging staff exchanges for the professional development of QUT staff, through work placements for extended times at McGill and Rensselaer Polytechnic.

In addition, structured studies of more than 15 United States, Canadian, and United Kingdom universities sustained ongoing learning personally, bringing many benefits from the insights of experienced international leaders in the field. I synthesized understandings from conversations, interviews, and studies within book chapters[89] and conference papers, distilling thoughts about best practices applicable to the QUT efforts. With benchmarking being a hot topic at the time, at least from the point of view of accountancy baselining, the focus of these ongoing studies on the benchmarking of service processes to deliver substantial improvement seemed to capture the interest of the far more experienced overseas advancement leaders. The President of the international professional body CASE (The Council for the Advancement and Support of Education) invited my sharing thoughts from these studies in Washington DC with leaders of advancement, whom he selected from leading North American universities.

Integrative Years

By 1995, QUT's institutional leaders were considering steps for a third comprehensive campaign, to build the fundraising further. To help prepare QUT, I made a study tour of some accomplished advancement operations in the United States, documenting what was pertinent from North American experience for tackling the next level of ambitions for the university. After setting initial preparations in place for the university to be able to conduct the next campaign, I decided it was the right time to leave QUT after more than two decades, for a position in the United States.

With thousands of accredited colleges or universities and 1.5 million registered nonprofit organizations in the United States, the challenges and competition to raise funds within the so-called third sector are substantial. Even in some well-established institutions, confusions and inaction abound. Disparate perspectives among trustees and senior managers of what enables fundraising that works for an organization will often limit success.

When first considering the possibility of seeking work in North America, a leading search consultant at a conference in Boston was especially helpful. After looking thoughtfully through my standard resume, she asked some questions about QUT, which she had never heard of, and what I'd done there. She then provided life changing advice to tell the story of the institution and my role leading the first successful development office through comprehensive fundraising campaigns in an Australian university.

Through the next two decades and more, during job interviews and consultancy pitches, when moving to a new position or working with clients, her initial advice helped tremendously. She advocated "going to where the tooth hurts," to diagnose doable challenges and make the changes needed to enhance relations with stakeholders and thereby improve fundraising results. Following more than a decade studying and applying best practices in institutional advancement, distilled from the efforts of well-established universities and colleges in the United States, United Kingdom, and Canada, the transition from Australia went smoothly.

Range of Experiences

In North America, the financially most able tend to live and work in interesting locations, requiring travel through the northwest, west coast, northeast, and southeast states, and sometimes internationally. Unexpected delights occur during travels, like the occasion that a board member of a consulting client set the venue for the board leadership retreat at the New York Yacht Club. After the session with the board members, he provided a guided tour. In the cavernous "Model Room" of the Beaux-Arts design building were 1,230 scale models of yachts dating from 1819, including the *America's Cup* winners and challengers—of which 147 are full-hull rigged models, many displayed side-by-side since the first race in 1851.

A role in institutional advancement can help advance a variety of innovative efforts. Working with people who lead innovation offers glimpses into strategies, talent, and accomplishments that shape world knowledge, nations, and lives. Frequently, the brilliant but often introspective scientists, researchers, and educators driving innovation firmly believe in conversation to stimulate creativity. Some convene symposia, meetings, and workshops with colleagues from throughout the world, or host events to share the significance of their discovery with the public, of all ages. These are stellar communicators with specific audiences, able to share their spectacular strength of mind to connect ideas not evident to others.

Common among many who advance innovation is to probe a single aspect of a challenge or theoretical problem, sometimes for months and years, until the way to shape the "new thing" emerges. In contrast, some policy decisions to implement change can happen at relative lightning-speed. The leader of the Office of Science and Technology Policy commented that at times he found sobering the speed with which decisions needed to be made on major issues in the White House, sometimes within half an hour. Then he looked at me intently, and said "…of course, I like to think it would be worse if I wasn't here to make input, because the decision would be made anyway."

In the United States and internationally, my professional activities have provided intriguing interactions to advance innovative efforts. Communication with senior leaders and researchers in the foremost companies, foundations, and government agencies has resulted in resources to advance endeavors in the arts, biomedicine, cybersecurity, engineering, hi-tech, power supply, and other fields. It is satisfying to match the interests of philanthropists and other community leaders with educators and researchers. And the organizations assembling innovative educators and researchers are stimulating places to work.

Personally, the developments in communication education in Australia enabled opportunities well beyond the expectations offered at age-18 by career-guidance advisers to become a cadet journalist or train as a schoolteacher. It is energizing to be able to secure substantial funding that helps to advance the efforts of some of the best minds in the world. Putting communication understandings into practice can offer a continuously expanding and exciting future.

Source Notes

1: Everything Felt New

1. Abbott, Malcolm and Chris Doucouliagos (2003), *The Changing Structure of Higher Education in Australia, 1949-2003*, Burwood, Vic: Deakin University, School of Accounting, Economics and Finance, School Working Papers, p. 16 https://www.deakin.edu.au/__data/assets/pdf_file/0006/402594/swp2003_07.pdf, Accessed August 17, 2022
2. Mabee, Keith (1976), "Where Will Public Relations Go from Here?" *Inter Connections: A Communication Journal*, 1(1), p. 26
3. Calhoun, Craig (2011), "Communication as Social Science (and More)," *International Journal of Communication*, 5, p. 1480 and p. 1484
4. Calhoun, p. 1480
5. Molloy, Bruce (1976), Introduction of Bruce Beresford, Brisbane, Qld, QIT
6. Maras, Steven (2004), "Thinking about the History of ANZCA: An Australian Perspective," *Australian Journal of Communication*, 31(2), pp. 13-51; Maras, Steven (2005), "Our Search for Meaning in Changing Times: An Interview with Bill Ticehust," edited transcript of interview on June 11, 2004, ANZCA Website, http://members.optusnet.com.au/~maras/ANZCAdossier/ticehurstinterview.html; Maras, Steven (2006), "The Emergence of Communication Studies in Australia as 'Curriculum Idea'," *Australian Journal of Communication*, 33(2,3), pp. 43-62, academia.edu/27033763/The_emergence_of_communication_studies_in_australia_as_curriculum_idea; Molloy, Bruce and June Lennie (1990), *Communication Studies in Australia: A Statistical Study of Teachers, Students and Courses in Australian Tertiary Institutions*, Brisbane, Qld: The Communication Centre, Queensland University of Technology, files.eric.ed.gov/fulltext/ED333518.pdf; Putnis, Peter (1993), "National Preoccupations and International Perspectives in Communication Studies in Australia," *Electronic Journal of Communication*, 3(3&4), pp. 1-15; Putnis, Peter (et. al.) (2002), *Communication and Media Studies in Australian Universities: An investigation into the growth, status, and future of this field of study*, Canberra: University of Canberra
7. Petelin, Roslyn (2013), "The *Australian Journal of Communication* (1976-2013): Tracing the Trajectory," *Review of Communication*, 13(4), p. 303, doi.org/10.1080/15358593.2013.867069
8. _____ (1972), *Handbook 1972: Queensland Institute of Technology*, Brisbane, Qld: QIT, https://digitalcollections.qut.edu.au/5693/1/Handbook_1972_QIT.pdf

9. _____ (1972)
10. Molloy, Bruce (2022), communication with author, August 14. I am grateful for Bruce's recollection and confirmation of some details of QIT.
11. Maras, Steven (2020), communication with author, 20 September
12. Molloy (2022)
13. Molloy (2022)
14. Molloy (2022)
15. Molloy (2022)
16. Miller, Rodney G. (1980a), "Developing Oral Communication in a Pluralistic Society: Rhetors and the Democratic Process," in Crocker, W.J. (Ed.), *Developing Oral Communication Competence*, Armidale, NSW: University of New England, pp. 86-7
17. Johnston, Jane (2013), "Breaking from Tradition: Developing Localised Discourses in an Emerging Global Discipline," *TEXT Special Issue 23, Textbooks and Educational Texts in the 21st Century: Writing, Publishing and Reading*, Horsley, Mike and Donna Lee Brien (Eds.), October,
    pp. 1-11 www.textjournal.com.au/speciss/issue23/Johnston.pdf
    Johnston, Jane and Jim Macnamara (2013), "Public Relations Literature and Scholarship in Australia: A Brief History of Change and Diversification," *PRism*, 10(1), pp. 1-16,
    opus.lib.uts.edu.au/bitstream/10453/30563/4/Public%20relations%20literature%20and%20scholarship%20in%20Australia.pdf;
18. O'Donnell, Penny and Margaret Van Heekeren (2015), "JERAA@40: Towards History of the Professional Association of Australian Journalism Academics," *Australian Journalism Review*, 37(2), pp. 1-22,
    core.ac.uk/download/pdf/212697411.pdf
19. Potts, J.D.S. (1977), "Public Relations Now," *Australian Scan: Journal of Human Communication*, 3, December, p. 4
20. O'Donnell and Van Heekeren, pp. 1-22
21. O'Donnell and Van Heekeren, p. 7
22. Pearson, Mark (2019), "D. Shelton A. Gunaratne (1940-2019)," *Journalism Education and Research Association of Australia website memorial*,
    jeraa.org.au/memoriam/dhavalasri-shelton-a-gunaratne-1940-2019/
23. Potts, p. 3

2: Into the Academy

24. Orwell, George (1981), "Politics and the English Language," *A Collection of Essays*, Orlando, FL: Harvest, pp. 156-71
25. Orwell, George (1954), "Principles of Newspeak," *Nineteen Eighty-Four*, Harmondsworth: Penguin, pp. 241-51
26. Ellul, Jacques (1965), *Propaganda: The Formation of Men's Attitudes*, New York: Knopf, p. 64
27. Ellul, p. 256
28. _____ (1987), "Premier Launches New QIT Look and Foundation Appeal," *Inside QIT*, No. 26, April 30, p. 1,
    https://digitalcollections.qut.edu.au/3469/1/QIT_April87_Iss26.pdf

29. Miller, Rodney G. and Roslyn Petelin (1985), "This and Now: Policy and Process for Developing Literacy," Brisbane, Qld: 4th National Australian Reading Association Conference, July 26
30. Miller and Petelin
31. _____ (1985), "21 Apple Awards Benefit Students," *The Courier-Mail*, July 9
32. Dixon, T.C. (1985), *Research and Consultancy Report 1985, Queensland Institute of Technology*, Brisbane, Qld: QIT, p. i
33. Freudenberg, Graham (1978), Seminar on Advanced Speech Writing at Queensland Institute of Technology (now Queensland University of Technology), Brisbane; see article (1978), 'Special Rapport', *The Courier-Mail*, May 6
34. Whitlam, E. Gough (1980), communication with author, September 15
35. Duce, Malcolm (2022), communication with author, August 14

3. National Professional Developments

36. Calhoun, p. 1484
37. Penman, Robyn (2012), "On Taking Communication Seriously," *Australian Journal of Communication*, 2012, 39(3), pp. 41-63, academia.edu/6487224/On_taking_communication_seriously_Penman, pp. 1-17
38. Löblich, M. & A. M. Scheu (2011), "Writing the History of Communication Studies: A Sociology of Science Approach," *Communication Theory*, 21, p.22
39. Stanfill, M. (2012), "Finding Birds of a Feather: Multiple Memberships and Diversity without Divisiveness in Communication Research," *Communication Theory*, 22, p. 1
40. Calhoun, p. 1485
41. Calhoun, p. 1485
42. Calhoun, p. 1488
43. _____ (2020), "Communicate," *Merriam-Webster*, merriam-webster.com/dictionary/communicate#h1 "Communis," Latdict, latin-dictionary.net/definition/11529/commune-communis Accessed July 22, 2020
44. Calhoun, p. 1485
45. _____ (1976), *Australian Scan: A Journal of Speech Communication*, 1(1), December. *SCAN* was derived as an acronym from *Speech Communication Association Notes*.
46. _____ (1976), *Inter Connections: A Communication Journal*, 1(1), December
47. Miller, Rodney G. (2012), communication with Roslyn Petelin, September
48. Miller, Rodney G. (2013), correspondence to Roslyn Petelin, in her "Editorial," *Australian Journal of Communication*, Vol 40 (3), p. iv
49. _____ (1977), *Conference on Interpersonal and Mass Communication, held at The New South Wales Institute of Technology, Sydney, 8th to 10th December: Conference Proceedings*, Kensington, NSW: Clarendon Press
50. Galloway, John J. (1977), "Communication Patterns and Communication Scholars: Invisible Colleges in the Emerging Communication Discipline," *Conference on Interpersonal and Mass Communication, held at The New South Wales Institute of Technology, Sydney, 8th to 10th December [1976]: Conference Proceedings*, Kensington, NSW: Clarendon Press, p. 154

51. Galloway, p. 157
52. Galloway, p. 157
53. Galloway, pp. 157-8
54. Miller, Rodney G. (Ed.) (1977), *Australian Scan: Journal of Speech Communication*, 1(2)
55. Crocker, W.J. (1977), "The Historical Present," *Australian Scan: Journal of Speech Communication*, 1(2), pp. 1-6
56. Irwin, Harry (1978), "An Innovative Approach to Interpersonal Communication for Management Students," *Australian Scan: Journal of Human Communication*, 4, August, pp. 45-56
57. Crocker, W.J. (Ed.) (1980), "List of Conference Participants," *Developing Oral Communication Competence*, Papers from an Invitation Conference Held to Discuss the Teaching of Oral Communication Skills to Children, Armidale: The University of New England, pp. 215-21

4. Communication Meaning

58. Ticehurst, Bill (2003) "Ten Years On–The Development of The Australian Communication Association". An ANZCA Dossier.Comp. Steven Maras. <http://www.anzca.net/dossier.htm> Accessed August 23, 2022
59. Garnham, Nicholas (1979), T.H.E.S., 15/4/77 Audio Visual Supplement, quoted in John Corner "Three Introductions to Communication Studies," *Communication Studies Bulletin*, 5, Summer, p. 29 (ISSN 0142-9655); Miller, Rodney G. (1980b), "Finding Communication Meaning in Australia," Raywood, SA: Inaugural Organizing Conference of the Australian Communication Association, May; For an attempt to standardize terminology in one model of communication see: Johnson, R.I. and Sager, J.C. (1980), "Standardization of Terminology in a Model of Communication," *International Journal of the Sociology of Language*, 23, pp. 81-104
60. Australian and New Zealand Association for the Advancement of Science (1980), Congress Proceedings, Section 33, Communication, in which a panel addressed the question of "Communication as a Discipline"
61. Blumler, Jay G. (1977), "The Emergence of Communication Studies," *Journal of Educational Television*, 3(1) Spring, p. 6
62. Stephen W. Littlejohn (1978), *Theories of Human Communication*, Columbus: Merrill, p. 24 and pp. 374-82
63. Johnson and Sager, pp. 81-104
64. Beattie, Earle (1982), Editorial, *Canadian Journal of Communication*, 8(2)
65. Tate, Eugene D., Andrew Osler, Gregory Fouts, Arthur Siegel (2000), "The Beginnings of Communication Studies in Canada: Remembering and Narrating the Past," *Canadian Journal of Communication*, 25(1), https://doi.org/10.22230/cjc.2000v25n1a1139
66. Pertisinidis, Sonia (2018), "The Crisis of Rhetoric in Australia," *ANU Reporter*, 49(4), https://reporter.anu.edu.au/crisis-rhetoric-australia
67. Tate, Osler, Fouts, and Siegel
68. Mayer, Henry (1976), *Media Probe*, (n.i.), p. 24, 154-Article Text-69-1-10-19760101.pdf; see also, on "media briefs," published in *Media Information Australia*, https://journals.sagepub.com/doi/abs/10.1177/1329878X7600100110

69. _____ (1982), *Australian Journal of Communication*, 1 & 2, January-December
70. Irwin, Harry and Elizabeth More (1983), 'Differing Perspectives and the Development of Communication Studies in Australia," in Smith III, Ted J. (Ed.), *Communication in Australia*, Warrnambool: Warrnambool Institute Press, pp. vii-viii
71. Bonney, W.L. (1983), "Two Approaches to Communication," in Smith III, Ted J. (Ed.), *Communication in Australia*, Warrnambool: Warrnambool Institute Press, pp. 1-5
72. _____ (1985), *Australian Journal of Communication*, 8, July-December: Irwin, Harry, "Interpersonal Communication Competence Revisited: Current Debates and Research Directions," pp. 25-31; Penman, Robyn, "A Rejoinder: Interpersonal Communication Competence in Another Frame," pp. 33-5; and, Irwin, Harry, "A Further Response: The Elusive Notion of Interpersonal Competence," pp. 37-40
73. _____ (1988), *Handbook, 1988: Queensland Institute of Technology*, Brisbane, Qld: QIT cms.qut.edu.au/__data/assets/pdf_file/0008/329057/quthb88.pdf
74. Molloy (2022)
75. _____ (1987), "Betty's Support for QIT Foundation Benefits Fundraising Profession," *Inside QIT*, No. 28, July 31, p. 2,
    https://digitalcollections.qut.edu.au/3469/3/QIT_July87_Iss28.pdf
76. Penman (2012), pp. 1-17; see also, Penman, Robyn (2014), "On Being Present and Participating: Projecting into Twenty-First-Century Media Life," Littlejohn, Stephen W. and Sheila McNamee (Eds.) *The Coordinated Management of Meaning: A Festschrift in Honor of W. Barnett Pearce*, Madison, NJ: Fairleigh Dickinson University Press, pp. 95-116
77. Penman (2012), p. 9
78. Penman (2012), p. 8
79. Penman (2012), p. 10
80. Penman (2012), p. 10
81. Penman (2012), p. 11; citing Cronen, V. (1995), "Practical Theory and the Tasks Ahead for Social Approaches to Communication," in Leeds-Hurwitz, W. (Ed.), *Social Approaches to Communication*, New York: Guilford, pp. 217-42; and Penman, Robyn (2000), *Reconstructing Communicating: Looking to a Future*, Mahwah NJ: Lawrence Erlbaum
82. Penman (2012), p. 8

5. Doing It

83. _____ (1986), "Communication Centre to Boost Consulting for Business, Govt," *Inside QIT*, No. 22, October 31, p. 2,
    https://digitalcollections.qut.edu.au/3468/8/QIT_Oct86_Iss22.pdf
84. Rice, Andy (2015), "America's Cup Legend Alan Bond Passes Away," *Boat*, June 8
85. Australian Government, Department of Employment, Education and Training (1988), *Higher Education: A Policy Statement* (Dawkins Report), Canberra: Australian Government; Australian Government, National Board of Employment, Education and Training (1989), *Report of the Task Force on Amalgamations in Higher Education*, Canberra: Australian Government

86. _____ (1987), "Miller Becomes First Assistant Dean (Dev.)," *Inside QIT*, No. 29, August 31, p. 2,
87. _____ (1990), "Appointments" Core faculty United States Indiana University Center of Philanthropy, *Business Queensland*, May 7, p. 25
88. _____ (1993), Awarded Certified Fund Raising Executive by United States National Society of Fund Raising Executives, *The Courier Mail*, May 15, p. 34
89. Miller, Rodney G. (1995a), "Improving Community Service: Strategic Cooperation through Communication," in Cushman, Donald Peter and Sarah Sanderson King (Eds.), *Communicating Organizational Change: A Management Perspective*, Albany, NY: State University of New York Press, pp. 65-81; (2001), "Beyond Benchmarking Institutional Advancement: Jump-start to Fund-raising Excellence," in Cushman, Donald Peter and Sarah Sanderson King (Eds.), *Excellence in Communicating Organizational Strategy*, Albany, NY: State University of New York Press, pp. 139-162

Bibliography

_____ (1972), *Handbook 1972: Queensland Institute of Technology*, Brisbane, Qld: QIT, https://digitalcollections.qut.edu.au/5693/1/Handbook_1972_QIT.pdf

_____ (1975), *Handbook 1974-1975: Queensland Institute of Technology*, Brisbane, Qld: QIT, https://digitalcollections.qut.edu.au/5695/2/Handbook_1974-75_QIT.pdf

_____ (1976), *Australian Scan: Journal of Speech Communication*, 1(1), December

_____ (1976), *Inter Connections: A Communication Journal*, 1(1), December

_____ (1977), *Conference on Interpersonal and Mass Communication, held at The New South Wales Institute of Technology, Sydney, 8th to 10th December [1976]: Conference Proceedings*, Kensington, NSW: Clarendon Press

_____ (1978), 'Special Rapport', *The Courier-Mail*, May 6

_____ (1981), *Australian Scan: Journal of Human Communication*, 9 & 10, December-November

_____ (1982), *Australian Journal of Communication*, 1 & 2, January-December

_____ (1983), *Australian Journal of Communication*, 3, January-June

_____ (1984), *Australian Journal of Communication*, 5 & 6, January-December

_____ (1985), *Australian Journal of Communication*, 8, July-December

_____ (1985), "21 Apple Awards Benefit Students," *The Courier-Mail*, July 9

_____ (1986), "Communication Centre to Boost Consulting for Business, Govt," *Inside QIT*, No. 22, October 31
https://digitalcollections.qut.edu.au/3468/8/QIT_Oct86_Iss22.pdf

_____ (1987), "Premier Launches New QIT Look and Foundation Appeal," *Inside QIT*, No. 26, April 30
https://digitalcollections.qut.edu.au/3469/1/QIT_April87_Iss26.pdf

_____ (1987), "Betty's Support for QIT Foundation Benefits Fundraising Profession," *Inside QIT*, No. 28, July 31,
https://digitalcollections.qut.edu.au/3469/3/QIT_July87_Iss28.pdf

_____ (1987), "Miller Becomes first Assistant Dean (Dev.)," *Inside QIT*, No. 29, August 31

_____ (1988), *Handbook, 1988: Queensland Institute of Technology*, Brisbane, Qld: QIT, cms.qut.edu.au/__data/assets/pdf_file/0008/329057/quthb88.pdf

_____ (1990), "Appointments" Core Faculty United States Indiana University Center of Philanthropy," *Business Queensland*, May 7, p. 25

_____ (1993), Awarded Certified Fund Raising Executive by United States National Society of Fund Raising Executives, *The Courier Mail*, May 15, p. 34

_____ (2020), "Communicate," *Merriam-Webster*, merriam-webster.com/dictionary/communicate#h1;

"Communis," Latdict, latin-dictionary.net/definition/11529/commune-communis

Abbott, Malcolm and Chris Doucouliagos (2003), *The Changing Structure of Higher Education in Australia, 1949-2003*, Burwood, Vic: Deakin University, School of Accounting, Economics and Finance, School Working Papers, https://www.deakin.edu.au/__data/assets/pdf_file/0006/402594/swp2003_07.pdf

Australian Government, Department of Employment, Education and Training (1988), *Higher Education: A Policy Statement* (Dawkins Report), Canberra: Australian Government

Australian Government, National Board of Employment, Education and Training (1989), *Report of the Task Force on Amalgamations in Higher Education*, Canberra: Australian Government

Australian and New Zealand Association for the Advancement of Science (1980), Congress Proceedings, Section 33, Communication, Adelaide, SA, in which a panel addressed the question of "Communication as a Discipline"

Barr, Trevor (1977), *Reflections of Reality: The Media in Australia*, Adelaide: Rigby

Beattie, Earle (1982), Editorial, *Canadian Journal of Communication*, 8(2)

Blumler, Jay G. (1977), "The Emergence of Communication Studies," *Journal of Educational Television*, 3(1) Spring, pp. 3-7

Bonney, W.L. (1983), "Two Approaches to Communication," in Smith III, Ted J. (Ed.), *Communication in Australia*, Warrnambool: Warrnambool Institute Press, pp. 1-5

Calhoun, Craig (2011), "Communication as Social Science (and More)," *International Journal of Communication*, 5, pp. 1479-96
https://www.researchgate.net/publication/286053816_Communication_as_Social_Science_and_More

Crocker, W.J. (1977), "The Historical Present," *Australian Scan: Journal of Speech Communication*, 1(2), pp. 1-6

Crocker, W.J. (Ed.) (1980), "List of Conference Participants," *Developing Oral Communication Competence*, Papers from an Invitation Conference Held to Discuss the Teaching of Oral Communication Skills to Children, Armidale: The University of New England, pp. 215-21

Cronen, V. (1995), "Practical Theory and the Tasks Ahead for Social Approaches to Communication," in W. Leeds-Hurwitz (Ed.), *Social Approaches to Communication*, New York: Guilford, pp. 217-42

Dixon, T.C. (1985), *Research and Consultancy Report 1985, Queensland Institute of Technology*, Brisbane, Qld: QIT

Duce, Malcolm (2022), communication with author, August 14

Edgar, Patricia (1975), "Directions in Mass Communication Research," *Australian and New Zealand Journal of Sociology*, 11(2), pp. 21-7

Ellul, Jacques (1965), *Propaganda: The Formation of Men's Attitudes*, New York: Knopf

Galloway, John J. (1977), "Communication Patterns and Communication Scholars: Invisible Colleges in the Emerging Communication Discipline," *Conference on Interpersonal and Mass Communication*, held at The New South Wales Institute of Technology,

Sydney, 8th to 10th December [1976]: Conference Proceedings, Kensington, NSW: Clarendon Press, pp. 153-63

Garnham, Nicholas (1979), T.H.E.S., 15/4/77 Audio Visual Supplement, quoted in John Corner "Three Introductions to Communication Studies," *Communication Studies Bulletin*, 5, Summer

Hodge, Robert (1982), "Culture as Communication: Towards a Theoretical Basis for Communication Studies," *Australian Journal of Communication*, 1 & 2, January-December, pp. 76-83

Irwin, Harry (1978), "An Innovative Approach to Interpersonal Communication for Management Students," *Australian Scan: Journal of Human Communication*, 4, August, pp. 45-56

Irwin, Harry and Elizabeth More (1983), 'Differing Perspectives and the Development of Communication Studies in Australia," in Smith III, Ted J. (Ed.), *Communication in Australia*, Warrnambool: Warrnambool Institute Press, pp. vii-viii

Irwin, Harry (1985), "Interpersonal Communication Competence Revisited: Current Debates and Research Directions," *Australian Journal of Communication*, 8, July-December, pp. 25-31 and "A Further Response: The Elusive Notion of Interpersonal Competence," pp. 37-40

Johnson, R.I. and J, C. Sager (1980), "Standardization of Terminology in a Model of Communication," *International Journal of the Sociology of Language*, 23, pp. 81-104

Johnston, Jane (2013), "Breaking from Tradition: Developing Localised Discourses in an Emerging Global Discipline," *TEXT Special Issue 23, Textbooks and Educational Texts in the 21st Century: Writing, Publishing and Reading*, Horsley, Mike and Donna Lee Brien (Eds.), October, pp. 1-11 www.textjournal.com.au/speciss/issue23/Johnston.pdf

Johnston, Jane and Jim Macnamara (2013), "Public Relations Literature and Scholarship in Australia: A Brief History of Change and Diversification," *PRism*, 10(1), pp. 1-16, opus.lib.uts.edu.au/bitstream/10453/30563/4/Public%20relations%20literature%20and%20scholarship%20in%20Australia.pdf;

King, Noel and Stephen Muecke (1984), "Caught between Two Paradigms: Communication Studies in Australia," *Australian Journal of Communication*, 5 & 6, pp. 1-2

Kress, Gunther (1983), "Directions in Communication Studies," *Australian Journal of Communication*, 4, July-December, pp. 1-6

Lewis, Glen (1982), "The Anglo-American Influence on Australian Communication Education," *Australian Journal of Communication*, 1 & 2, January-December, pp. 14-20

Littlejohn, Stephen W. (1978), *Theories of Human Communication*, Columbus: Merrill

Mabee, Keith (1976), "Where Will Public Relations Go from Here?" *Inter Connections: A Communication Journal*, 1(1), pp. 26-8

Maras, Steven (2004), "Thinking about the History of ANZCA: An Australian Perspective," *Australian Journal of Communication*, 31(2), pp. 13-51

Maras, Steven (2005), "Our Search for Meaning in Changing Times: An Interview with Bill Ticehust," edited transcript of interview on June 11, 2004, ANZCA Website, http://members.optusnet.com.au/~maras/ANZCAdossier/ticehurstinterview.html

Maras, Steven (2006), "The Emergence of Communication Studies in Australia as 'Curriculum Idea'," *Australian Journal of Communication*, 33(2,3), pp. 43-62, academia.edu/27033763/The_emergence_of_communication_studies_in_australia _as_curriculum_idea

Maras, Steven (2020), communication with author, September 20

Mayer, Henry (1976), *Media Probe*, (n.i.), p. 24, 154-Article Text-69-1-10-19760101.pdf; see also, on "media briefs," published in *Media Information Australia*, https://journals.sagepub.com/doi/abs/10.1177/1329878X7600100110

Miller, Rodney G. (1980a), "Developing Oral Communication in a Pluralistic Society: Rhetors and the Democratic Process," in Crocker, W.J. (Ed.), *Developing Oral Communication Competence*, Armidale, NSW: University of New England, pp. 85-91

Miller, Rodney G. (1980b), "Finding Communication Meaning in Australia," Inaugural Organizing Conference of Australian Communication Association, Raywood, SA

Miller, Rodney G. and Roslyn Petelin (1985), "This and Now: Policy and Process for Developing Literacy," Brisbane, Qld: 4th National Australian Reading Association Conference, July 26

Miller, Rodney G. (1995), "Improving Community Service: Strategic Cooperation through Communication," in Cushman, Donald Peter and Sarah Sanderson King (Eds.), *Communicating Organizational Change: A Management Perspective*, Albany, NY: State University of New York Press, pp. 65-81

Miller, Rodney G. (2001), "Beyond Benchmarking Institutional Advancement: Jump-start to Fund-raising Excellence," in Cushman, Donald Peter and Sarah Sanderson King (Eds.), *Excellence in Communicating Organizational Strategy*, Albany, NY: State University of New York Press, pp. 139-162

Miller, Rodney G. (2012), communication with Roslyn Petelin, September

Miller, Rodney G. (2013), communication with Roslyn Petelin, for "Editorial," *Australian Journal of Communication*, Vol 40 (3), p. iv

Mohan, Terry (1977), "Mass Media and Cultural Studies," *Conference on Interpersonal and Mass Communication, held at The New South Wales Institute of Technology, Sydney, 8th to 10th December [1976]: Conference Proceedings*, Kensington, NSW: Clarendon Press, pp. 350-80

Molloy, Bruce and June Lennie (1990), *Communication Studies in Australia: A Statistical Study of Teachers, Students and Courses in Australian Tertiary Institutions*, Brisbane, Qld: The Communication Centre, Queensland University of Technology, files.eric.ed.gov/fulltext/ED333518.pdf

Molloy, Bruce (2022), communication with author, August 14

O'Donnell, Penny and Margaret Van Heekeren (2015), "JERAA@40: Towards History of the Professional Association of Australian Journalism Academics," *Australian Journalism Review*, 37(2), pp. 1-22, core.ac.uk/download/pdf/212697411.pdf

Orwell, George (1981), "Politics and the English Language," *A Collection of Essays*, Orlando, FL: Harvest, pp. 156-71 [first published 1946]

Orwell, George (1954), "Principles of Newspeak," *Nineteen Eighty-Four*, Harmondsworth: Penguin, pp. 241-51 [first published 1949]

Pearson, Mark (2019), "D. Shelton A. Gunaratne (1940-2019)," *Journalism Education and Research Association of Australia website memorial*, jeraa.org.au/memoriam/dhavalasri-shelton-a-gunaratne-1940-2019/

Penman, Robyn (1982), "Problems in Human Communication Studies: Another Argument," *Australian Journal of Communication*, 1 & 2, January-December, pp. 52-7

Penman, Robyn (1985), "A Rejoinder: Interpersonal Communication Competence in Another Frame," *Australian Journal of Communication*, 8, July-December, pp. 33-5

Penman, Robyn (2000), *Reconstructing Communicating: Looking to a Future*, Mahwah NJ: Lawrence Erlbaum

Penman, Robyn (2012), "On Taking Communication Seriously," *Australian Journal of Communication*, 2012, 39(3), pp. 41-63, academia.edu/6487224/On_taking_communication_seriously_Penman, pp. 1-17

Penman, Robyn (2014), "On Being Present and Participating: Projecting into Twenty-First-Century Media Life," Littlejohn, Stephen W. and Sheila McNamee (Eds.) *The Coordinated Management of Meaning: A Festschrift in Honor of W. Barnett Pearce*, Madison, NJ: Fairleigh Dickinson University Press, pp. 95-116

Pertisinidis, Sonia (2018), "The Crisis of Rhetoric in Australia," *ANU Reporter*, 49(4), https://reporter.anu.edu.au/crisis-rhetoric-australia

Petelin, Roslyn (2013), "*The Australian Journal of Communication* (1976-2013): Tracing the Trajectory," *Review of Communication*, 13(4), pp. 302-15

Potts, J.D.S. (1977), "Public Relations Now," *Australian Scan: Journal of Human Communication*, 3, December, pp. 1-6

Putnis, Peter (1993), "National Preoccupations and International Perspectives in Communication Studies in Australia," *Electronic Journal of Communication*, 3(3&4), pp. 1-15

Putnis, Peter (et. al.) (2002), *Communication and Media Studies in Australian Universities: An investigation into the growth, status, and future of this field of study*, Canberra: University of Canberra

Rice, Andy (2015), "America's Cup Legend Alan Bond Passes Away," *Boat*, June 8

Rogers, E.M. and S.H. Chaffee (1983), "Communication as an Academic Discipline," *Journal of Communication*, 33(3), pp. 18-30

Stanfill, M. (2012), "Finding Birds of a Feather: Multiple Memberships and Diversity without Divisiveness in Communication Research," *Communication Theory*, 22, pp. 1-24

Tate, Eugene D., Andrew Osler, Gregory Fouts, Arthur Siegel (2000), "The Beginnings of Communication Studies in Canada: Remembering and Narrating the Past," *Canadian Journal of Communication*, 25(1) https://doi.org/10.22230/cjc.2000v25n1a1139

Ticehurst, Bill, (2003), "Ten Years On–The Development of The Australian Communication Association". An ANZCA Dossier.Comp. Steven Maras. <http://www.anzca.net/dossier.htm>

Whitlam, E. Gough (1980), communication with author, September 15

Acknowledgments

My thanks go to family, friends, and former colleagues for many enjoyable life experiences. For contributions or contact during the writing of this booklet, I am grateful to Phil Crowe, Halina Duce, Malcolm Duce OBE, Harry Irwin, The Hon Michael Kirby AC CMG, Patricia McCarthy, John Matthews, Bruce Molloy, Roslyn Petelin, and Bill Ticehurst–with extra appreciation for excusing the long interval between contacts, while I pursued adventures in the United States.

My special thanks to Steven Maras for his detailed early suggestions on some excerpts in the booklet, as well as for his efforts over so many years to put together excellent chronicles on communication education in Australia. As an early participant in the development of what is now the *Australian and New Zealand Communication Association*, I am grateful for his thoughtful commentaries, which will be valuable to the generations shaping Australian communication education into the future.

I also extend thanks to the many people who, over many years, have contributed to the advancement of communication education and offer apologies for not being able to mention everyone. Every effort was made to recall accurately details and interpretations from times long past, and I am responsible for deficiencies that remain. Thank you to all who took the trouble to reply to my inquiries, whether or not they were able to help.

As always, very much appreciated are my wife, family, and friends near and far, who with understanding, good humor, and patience enable my writing.

About the Author

Rodney G. Miller writes about communication. He is published by the State University of New York Press, other universities, and The Royal Society of Queensland, with early writing published in *The Australian* newspaper.

His book *Australians Speak Out: Persuasive Language Styles* illustrates the persuasive strength of leaders who use ordinary words in extraordinary ways to make democracy thrive. It is the first detailed assessment of the public communication of these notable leaders from the 1890s to modern times. *Communication Essays* details insights and priorities to seek understanding, relationship, and action through systematic, personal communication. Seven provocative essays, written through three decades, explore ways to strengthen public discourse in a democracy and the interaction of an organization with the community–including ground-breaking study of institutional advancement leaders at some of the most successful universities in the world.

While teaching communication at Queensland University of Technology (QUT), he established The Communication Institute, founding and editing the *Australian Journal of Communication* for over a decade. He has since led external relations and the advancement of innovative education at QUT and universities in the United States and internationally, also consulting on communication, serving as adjunct faculty in fundraising at the Indiana University-Purdue University center on philanthropy, and chairing or serving on the governing boards of educational, professional, and community organizations.

Also by the author

Communication Essays
Australians Speak Out: Persuasive Language Styles
Finding a Future

Website: communicator.rodney-miller.com